AHA MOMENTS

of Sudden Realization, Inspiration, and Insight from 26 Professional Men

Quentin Newhouse Jr., PhD
Editor

All rights reserved. No part of this publication may be reproduced, stored in a retrieval system, or transmitted, in any form or by any means, electronic, mechanical, photocopying, recording, or otherwise, without the prior written consent of the author.

Copyright © 2017 by Quentin Newhouse Jr., PhD
All rights reserved.

Green Ivy Publishing
1 Lincoln Centre
18W140 Butterfield Road
Suite 1500
Oakbrook Terrace IL 60181-4843
www.greenivybooks.com

ISBN: 978-1-946775-17-7
Ebook: 978-1-946775-18-4

Contents

SOURCES OF *A-HA MOMENTS* CONTRIBUTORS	vii
Dedication	x
Introduction	1
A-ha Moments!	
of Sudden Realization, Inspiration, and Insight	
from 26 Professional Men	
Quentin Newhouse Jr., PhD, CPC, PCC (Editor)	1
And He Shall Be Like a Tree	
Quentin Newhouse Jr.- Montreal, Quebec	4
Your Burdens Become Your Blessings	
*Clint Boyd Jr.-*Hendersonville, Tennessee (deceased)	15
Looking Back	
*Wilbert Haywood Grandy Sr.-*Washington, DC	24
From Electronics to Evangelism	
*Pastor Joseph Hovsepian-*Montreal, Quebec	31
When I Look in the Mirror	
*Bruce A. Herman-*Lafayette, California	36
A-ha Moments	
*Andreas Deligeorge-*Montreal, Quebec	46
Foundation, Motivation, Education, and Favor	
*Rick Sinkfield, AIA-*San Antonio, Texas	56

Purpose, Responsibility, Mentorship and Contribution
  Louis O. Biggers-California   68

The Choices We Make
  James T. Worthy-Toledo, Ohio   75

A-ha Moments
  Ricardo McCrae-Toronto, Ontario   80

A-ha Moments
  Pharaoh Freeman-Montreal, Quebec   91

My A-ha Moment
  Marc Garfinkle-Springfield, New Jersey   97

My Name is Howie
  Howard Blessing, DMD-Walla Walla, Washington   104

A-HA!!!!!!
SO THAT'S HOW IT ALL WORKS
  Bart Gullong-Jupiter, Florida   111

My **A-ha** Moments
  Dr. H.E. "Doc" Holliday, Ph.D. -Kennesaw, Georgia   117

The Heart of the Decision
  Earle Maiman-Cincinnati, Ohio   127

Unexpected Moments in an Academic Life
  Charles S. Taylor, PhD-Yellow Springs, Ohio   134

Listen to Your Heart
  Steve Brandt-Pleasant Garden, North Carolina   143

My **A-ha** Moment
Sudden Realization, Inspiration and Insight
   Ricardo Anderson, PhD-Indianapolis, Indiana   *150*

Follow Your Passion—It Is Your Ticket to Happiness
   Barry D. Shur, PhD-Pasadena, California   *157*

My **A-ha** Moments
   Timothy Creel, MBA, MS-Murfreesboro, Tennessee   *165*

The Resilient Life
   Dr. Wayne Norton-Tyro, Kansas   *171*

A-ha Moments
   Sean Evers, PhD-Manasquan, New Jersey   *185*

Once a Dork, Always a Dork
   Joseph Singleton-Dayton, Ohio   *195*

A-ha Moments
   Michael LeClair-Yamhill, Oregon   *212*

Moments on the Voyage to Manhood
   Gary Carson, JD-Kerrville, Texas   *218*

SOURCES OF A-HA MOMENTS CONTRIBUTORS

High School (1964–1967)

Wilbert Haywood Grandy Sr. (father of the best friend of the editor in Washington, DC), retired pharmacist

Rick Sinkfield (high school colleague), retired architect

College (1967–1971)

Dr. Earl Holliday, college professor

James T. Worthy, Vietnam veteran and retired fireman

College Fraternity Brothers – older (1967–1970)

Dr. Howie Blessing, retired dentist

Bart Gullong, consultant/businessman

Dr. Gary Carson, oil and land gas professional

Dr. Charles Taylor, professor emeritus

Earle Maiman, retired attorney

College Fraternity Brothers – same age (1967–1971)

Dr. Barry Shur, retired dean

Dr. Sean Evers, psychologist in private practice

Steve Brandt, advertising professional

<u>College Fraternity Brothers – younger (1968–1971)</u>

Marc Garfinkle, attorney

Bruce Herman, president, international distilleries

Michael LeClair, postmaster, former mayor, former municipal judge, musician

<u>Friends from Nashville, Tennessee, USA (2001–2006)</u>

Clint Boyd, businessman

Timothy Creel, accounting professor and coworker

<u>Canadian Influences (2007–Present)</u>

Joseph Hovsepian, pastor and businessman

Andreas Deligeorge, businessman

Pharaoh Freeman, businessman

Ricardo McCrae, businessman

LinkedIn Contacts (2013–2014)

Dr. Ricardo Anderson, professor/school administrator

Dr. Wayne Norton, pastor

Louis Biggers, businessman

Joe Singleton, aeronautical sciences and management professional

Dedication

There are so many men who inspired this book and bare acknowledging. In the interest of time, focus, and relevance, I will be rather specific in this dedication. The list is long, although not exhaustive. As a note, all of these men would have been authors featured in this book had they been living and/or were willing. In two cases, they are indeed *A-ha Moments* authors.

My love of God and respect for the life, teachings, death, and resurrection of Jesus are foremost in my model of manhood. My father, Quentin Newhouse Sr., who died in 1992, provided me with strength of character, determination, spiritual awareness, and courage. I will be forever grateful for the honor he gave me by giving me his name. I watched him battle life's challenges as a black man 1) working two and often three full-time jobs to feed his family but never really achieving all he felt capable of achieving, 2) battling pancreatic cancer and undergoing kidney dialysis while never neglecting his spiritual assignments as a deacon at the Shiloh Baptist Church in Washington, DC, and 3) supporting my mother in raising me and my two sisters, and in her own personal and professional interests. I have included a picture of my dad and me (I was about 2. He still has my back and I feel his strength in my everyday life.)

Jacob Napier was a Muslim barber in Washington, DC, who taught me about compassion and service to others. "Mr. Jake on 13th and H St. NE", as people called him, wore a bow tie and white shirt to work every day. Mr. Jake asked me to be his cashier on weekends throughout my high school years and whenever I was home from college. Mr. Jake also taught me a lesson because he was willing to help me get a barber's license, but I was too narrow-minded and focused on my education to see what he was doing. There were many days, during and after college, when I was quite hungry and lacked money, that my craft as a licensed barber would have given me the means to live better.

Although younger than me, Clint Boyd, one of the *A-ha Moments* authors, who sent me his material on August 27 and died around September 8, will always serve as a model of fatherhood and brotherly love. The concept of being evenly yoked was evident between him and his wife, Elaine, and I thank both of them for showing me how it is done.

I also want to dedicate this book to my Canadian pastor, Joseph Hovsepian, who fortunately was one of the first *A-ha Moments* authors to complete his chapter and make a financial contribution. He is affectionately known as "Pastor Joseph." For seven years, I have watched the 70-plus-year-old Pastor Joseph serve as a full-time volunteer pastor of Temple Baptist Church, here in Montreal, Quebec. He is always available to his members and provides spiritual support and development. Pastor Joseph delivers what I call "ouch sermons." He has no problem boldly quoting scripture regarding God's promises and wrath for disobedience. There were times when the pews were not as full as he wanted, probably because people did not want to hear what God had placed in his heart and mouth to say, which would have been perceived as quite unpopular.

Pastor Joseph is a successful and well-respected businessman with an electronics shop in Montreal. He is a husband to his wife of more than 50 years. He is a father and a grandfather. The church is phenomenal in itself. It has fewer than 70 members, but it supports three overseas ministries in Bangladesh, the Philippines, and Armenia. Pastor Joseph has quietly supported many smaller and larger projects, helping in whatever means necessary. In addition, Pastor Joseph's inspired leadership is evident in a vibrant Men's Fellowship, which has existed for more than 20 years and where often 20–35 men and boys from age 7 to over age 80 meet for two hours on a Saturday to discuss spiritual issues. Members of this group and volunteers have been singing *a capella* for the church on many occasions for the past three years. His devotion to God, consistency, resolve, and kindness have been inspirational to me. Although he is only ten years older than I am, I see him as my spiritual father and earthly brother.

Introduction

A-ha Moments!
of Sudden Realization, Inspiration, and Insight
from 26 Professional Men

Quentin Newhouse Jr., PhD, CPC, PCC (Editor)

The quest for becoming a man can arguably be perceived as more difficult now than ever before in history. The rising prominence of women with power and authority in the workplace and the home (and the reality that they do not need a man to provide for or protect them), the blurring of gender roles and identity, and the breakdown of family roles and functions further complicate this process. Many boys discover their manhood only through women's eyes, after going to prison, surviving all kinds of addictions, being chronically unemployable, by yielding to unethical peer pressure, from exposure to and involvement in gangs, through distorted and biased perspectives, and often through trial and much error.

Each year there is a new book chronicling the rites of passage that boys should take in approaching and embracing manhood. Each year there are more single-parented or psychologically fatherless boys who do not have the guidance or wisdom of a steady dad, or even a willing male role model other than the negative or unachievable ones seen in the media or in their neighborhoods.

When these books or efforts on passage appear, they tend to

chronicle the efforts of famous men who beat the odds and excelled to the "highest heights." We might dream that we can make similar achievements, but many of us do not have the unique conflagration of providence, luck, dedication, and grit that often characterize these men. What seems more feasible are the millions of ordinary men who are not famous, according to media standards (as we like to call them, "below the radar"), who are successful in what they have achieved in their lives. These extraordinary, unsung heroes often live and die, unheralded, without the opportunity to tell their stories. Their journeys, successes, and setbacks are unchronicled but just as inspiring as the more famous ones, and their stories deserve to be told. Several of these men are in the latter days of their careers and lives, but their wisdom is priceless for a practical and achievable understanding of what it means to be a man.

This book chronicles the *A-ha Moments*, or turning points, revelations, and insights in each of the selected men's lives, irrespective of when they realized what it meant to be a man and moved directly on that journey. These moments may be psychological, sociological, professional, or spiritual, but we are convinced they will be inspiring and educational. Men of all ages will be enriched by the collective wisdom of men of all races, ages, and disciplines that should better improve the transition to "manhood," whatever that means these days.

My initial goal was to write the book alone. I approached a colleague of mine with whom I resonated from my IPEC coaching training. He withdrew co-editing the book because of his professional commitments, but I decided to make a list of the men who had influenced and impressed me throughout my life. I had more than 40 men on that list. Several dropped out due to time constraints, one was threatened to be sued by his family if he shared his past, and others never responded to my initial appeal. It took nine months to assemble these 25 stories.

I decided that rather than write the book alone, throwing one "rock" that young men and readers could duck or discount, I

OF SUDDEN REALIZATION, INSPIRATION, AND INSIGHT FROM 26 PROFESSIONAL MEN

would throw multiple "rocks" or stories that would be impossible to duck, defer, deflect, or deny. I have not seen many of these men in 40 or more years; however, whenever I approached them, they responded eagerly and willingly. I lived in a fraternity house with many of these men for the four years I was in college and saw them every day in every way. My criteria for selection were successful but humble men who impressed me by being "real men" who would tell their stories with candor, wisdom, and passion. I am thankful that all of the men stepped up and wrote impassioned and real stories that should be "undodgeable," even if a hybrid of reading and applying two or more stories is the outcome. I have been blessed by rekindling old friendships, making new ones, and even encouraging the *A-ha Moments* men to network with each other. These men are from all colors and races—black, white, everyone. They are distributed throughout the US and Canada, from a 30-year-old businessman who designed my business cards and redesigned my website to the 93-year-old father of my best friend in Washington, DC.

Thank you, gentlemen. You exceeded my expectations and I am proud to represent you by championing the collection and distribution of this effort. To God be the glory for the victories he has won.

As the editor, I am humbled by the depth and breadth of experiences these men brought to this project. We took notes as we read these short stories and their bios. We only hope and pray that God will enrich what was placed in our spirits to do. Women will also benefit from reading this book to better understand how men think. There are several themes that will emerge in reading all of them, and these need not be stated, but are evident in the hearts, minds, and behaviors of these unsung heroes.

And He Shall Be Like a Tree

Quentin Newhouse Jr.

Throughout my life, whenever I met some of my geographically closest and more distant relatives (whether at a family reunion or elsewhere), I noted that most of the Newhouse clan are not quite 6 feet tall. Although not a midget, I was called short by many of my contemporaries. My A-ha Moments are ones of stature, because as an adolescent, I overcame many challenges to my perception of my physical height. My story also resonates around my two favorite Bible scriptures, Luke 2:52 ("*and Jesus grew in wisdom and stature, and in favor with God and man*") and Psalm 1:3 ("*and he shall be like a tree, planted by the rivers of waters*") as my focal points.

I noticed that during a violent storm, seemingly strong and large trees are uprooted. The key term is "uprooted." I also noticed that those trees with deeper roots are less likely to fall over. This essay and my life are examples of deeper roots—understanding my family and myself—that have anchored me by the "rivers of water" in my life.

Dictionary.com defines stature in the following way:

1. *the height of a human or animal body*

2. *the height of any object*

3. *degree of development attained; level of achievement* (http://dictionary.reference.com/browse/stature?s=t). The first usage was in 1250–1300 AD, and the origin is Middle English, Old French

OF SUDDEN REALIZATION, INSPIRATION, AND INSIGHT FROM 26 PROFESSIONAL MEN

(*stature*), and Latin (*statura*).

I would actually adhere to the British definition of stature:

1. *the height of something, esp a person or animal when standing*

2. *the degree of development of a person: the stature of a champion*

3. *intellectual or moral greatness: a man of stature* (http://dictionary.reference.com/browse/stature?s=t)

As I compose this story, I would be remiss not to acknowledge some of the women who have also contributed to my quest for manhood. I hail from a long line of strong, statured women, including my maternal grandmother, who owned a grocery store in Texas in the 1940s, moved to Washington, DC, in 1949 to assist our family in raising me and my two sisters (she was my only babysitter), and was noted as a champion of the installation of lights on a local playground so that children could play at night.

Without my mother, this story would be quite moot. She inspired me in so many ways. She was a strong, opinionated woman who was described by one of our family pastors as "frankly brutal and brutally frank." I have her tongue, and I pray often that God will keep it in check. I have enough material to write at least two books about her, but it is relevant that she completed her bachelor's degree at 58 years old, her master's at 60, and a PhD at 66. She pledged the Delta Sigma Theta sorority at 70 and wore stiletto heels until she was 78, when she married a 55-year-old man. These and other women helped me to unlock the "feminine" side of me (compassion, gentleness, or intuition) that has provided stronger roots in my maturing as a tree, and this should not go unnoticed.

My story also takes on additional genealogical relevance in that I can only trace my family back two generations. My grandfather (my dad's dad) was a farmer in Texas. My father was a janitor and a clothes presser. He said that he dropped out of Howard University's School of Pharmacy so that he could feed my stay-at-home mother, my two sisters, and me. He worked two and sometimes three full-time jobs to provide for us, and I told him he had earned a PhD (perfectly honorable dad), after I earned my academic one, for his sacrifices on my behalf.

My father was a quiet man of few words. My mother called him "honey." He let his behavior speak for him. I never saw him raise his voice to me, my mother, or my sisters. I never saw him drunk, high, or violent to any of us. I also never saw him confront my mother on any issue. In another *A-ha Moment*, when I was 18, I stopped blaming my parents for anything and began my journey to perfect the good and eliminate the bad socializations I received from them.

The summer of 1966 may have held many revelations for many people, but for me, it was the summer when I was 5'5" tall and most of my boyhood friends outgrew me by 4–8 inches. Mind you, it did not matter to me because at that age (17) I was taller than both of my parents; however, my cohorts thought it a constant joke to ask me when I would grow. They even picked me up one time and shook me, hoping that my legs would grow immediately. I decided to put an end to this madness. As I have always had a sharp tongue and a facility with words (which I got from my mother), I uttered this statement: "I would rather be my height and intelligent than tall and stupid." I believe that revelation worked because after that time, my height (now regarded as my maturing) was no longer an issue for me or my friends.

An even more interesting recent anecdote is a conversation I had in January 2015 with a high school friend who is about 6'4" tall. I told him that I took a picture with Dikembe Mutumbo, a 7-foot-plus former professional basketball player, and my friend remarked that because of the height differences, two pictures were probably taken. When I reminded him of my "short, intelligent, tall, stupid" comment, he laughed and promptly changed the subject. *Touché.*

My roots came from a small, humble family who lived in

OF SUDDEN REALIZATION, INSPIRATION, AND INSIGHT FROM 26 PROFESSIONAL MEN

Hallsville, Texas, or nearby. Many of my relatives are teachers, architects, linguists, and professional athletes. My father was one of ten children: six brothers and four sisters. I have many first and second cousins throughout that region, and the family reunions are testaments that the Newhouse family has attempted to establish and maintain stature in society.

This lineage of my forefathers, foremothers, and relatives has given me a rubric for how I live my life and how I have evaluated my A-ha Moments. I would summarize these guidelines as my attempts to share that men should grow in favor with God and man, purpose, wisdom, clarity of vision, and fearlessness.

I will not go any further in this essay until I step off of my soapbox for this "news flash." I am far from perfect and want to publicly apologize to anyone I may have ever offended in any way throughout my life (I have left my fair share of carnage in 65 years). I have fallen far short of the "glory of God" many times and have been embarrassed about those incidents. During those times, I did not stand tall at all and my lack of integrity was showing. I work harder to limit those incidents, but it bares saying at this juncture that I am hardly a saint. I want young men to know that I have sinned, and sin consistently, and always pray for forgiveness (as I just did publicly). I just showed my humility, transparency, and honesty with you. Another book I want to write would teach young men that there is nothing unmanly in saying "I am sorry," "I am lost," "I do not know," and "I love you." Having said that, I still want to share my story of stature with you.

Favor with God and man

Young men should assertively seek to know why they were created. We were all created for a reason. Luke 2:52 says that *Jesus grew in wisdom and stature, and in favor with God and man.* Growth says looking beyond oneself to a higher calling. All of us were created for a reason.

Favor is an interesting topic. There are biblical discussions of favoritism, grace, and mercy. Favor is positioning, respect, and regard. I may be part of the last generation that believed in "word of mouth" to transmit information and the "contract handshake." Recommendations as well as news once traveled faster and probably more reliably than the Internet through word of mouth. Entire neighborhoods would be alerted of an intruder within minutes and community resources would be employed to escort away or repel those persons. Reputations, rapport, and goodwill are also accompaniments of favor.

There was a time when a simple handshake was enough to close a business deal. One's word was one's bond. Now there are so many stipulations within a contract, you are really not sure what you have signed. We often utter vain promises we have no intention of keeping.

Purpose

If you believe in God, then creation becomes a more purposeful event. If not, then certainly one should not let the dash between the day one was born and the day one dies be the only event.

Growth requires progress and process. I have had *A-ha Moments* we called "time warps," where one could often observe cohorts who never changed over the years. They often had the same behaviors, patterns of doing or not doing things, and were the consummate procrastinators. If you visited them, they often hung out on the same corners where you left them twenty years ago, and they have no aspirations to leave there or change. Growth also means studying one's craft to master whatever you do for a living. To paraphrase Dr. Martin Luther King Jr., "If you are a trash man, be the best trash man you can be."

Wisdom

Growth also suggests maturity or wisdom, making the correct decisions at the appropriate time. The Bible states, "*When I became a man, I put away childish things*" (1 Corinthians 13:11). There may be some individuals who are chronologically considered men who are not. Actually, chronological age has little to do with manhood. Having children and not supporting them in all ways is not "manly." Verbally or physically abusing women is not "manly."

Another *A-ha Moment* that I have recounted numerous times during my teaching career is the "two minutes missing from my adolescence." I remember that, when I was 13, my father was with me at a social affair (church, if I remember correctly) and asked me to go and get something for him. I remember thinking "I am taller than him now, this is a good time to tell him no". I said "No, I do not want to get it now." I vaguely remember him looking at me in a way that I had never seen before. In retrospect, I believe he was prepared to kill me at that point. Suddenly, a curtain came over me and I remember waking up about two minutes later. My father was walking away from me. I interpreted that I fainted from the shock of believing that I was going to die at his hand. There was no pain, but I could not account for what happened. Most amazingly, thirty years later, in 1992, in the emergency room of a local hospital where my father had been taken when his temperature would not decrease, I asked him what had happened that "special day." The last smile I remember from my father (as he was actually dying) was his satisfaction of keeping the source of what happened from me. It worked, because from that time in my adolescence to the day he died, I respected his authority and power and to some degree feared my father. He re-established his position as the head of our household and as disciplinarian over me.

Many young men do not fear or respect any authority figures, whether parents, spiritual leaders, teachers or police officers. More recently, these confrontations between teenagers and these authority figures have not resulted in positive outcomes. The teenagers do not defer to the authority figures and police have the authority to use whatever force is necessary to "subdue the situation." I learned my lesson on stature that day, that no matter how tall I stood, my father would always stand above me.

Stature in this regard includes having principles to live by. Spiritual and moral principles are often taught during childhood, but certainly laws are set to be upheld. Infringing the law by indirect or direct means is not living up to what society expects of all its citizens, not just men. Once a boy becomes 18, society views his behavior in a different way. In fact, in the US, if a youth commits a crime at 14, he might be tried as an adult. Respect authority and the rights of others.

Clarity of Vision

More crucial is to assess what one is willing to die for. In 2015, wearing a Seattle Seahawks jersey in Green Bay, Wisconsin, might not be tactful or evidence of clear vision or discernment. Having lost the NFL Championship game, there are some die-hard fans who might resort to something more than saying "hello" in your interaction with them. It is rare that anyone has to test this principle, but few men are passionate about anything. Standing against the majority and the odds is another test of stature.

Finally, stature suggests stability, consistency, and fearlessness. Young men should look for opportunities to maintain a steady job, girlfriend, marriage, or set of friends. Being consistent means presenting a stable set of behaviors one can rely on and predict to some extent. Manhood should not be characterized as snap judgments and erratic behavior.

Being fearless means being able to focus oneself on a duty or task to the point that there are no perceived obstacles to get them completed. Fear is often characterized as false evidence appearing real. Being fearless also means stepping out of one's own comfort zone and engaging in some new and novel behavior.

In summary, my *A-ha Moments* reside around maintaining my relationship with God and the Bible as my moral compass, trying to practice some wisdom learned through personal and professional experiences, and to establish favor with my fellow humans.

As they say, if I could turn back time, a better answer to those taller friends who so willingly shook me would have been "I am standing like a tree, growing in wisdom and stature and favor with God and man."

Bio of Dr. Quentin Newhouse, Jr.

An accomplished executive coach, life coach, university professor and administrator, motivational speaker, and author, Dr. Quentin Newhouse Jr. has enjoyed a tremendously successful career filled with several significant achievements. Throughout his brilliant professional career, Dr. Newhouse has routinely demonstrated passion, vision, dedication, and diligence.

Drawing upon his wealth of knowledge, acquired over the course of his incredibly impressive career, Dr. Newhouse is the president of Q Newhouse Structured Coaching Strategies, Inc. (QNSCS), a Canadian corporation. Through QNSCS, Dr. Newhouse has completed more than 2,000 paid hours for 75-plus clients in North America, Australia, and Thailand. QNSCS empowers individuals and organizations with life, career, and organizational skills to promote happiness, productivity, and success, both personally and professionally. QNSCS is a member of the Montreal Canada Board of Trade and Biz Montreal (B to B).

OF SUDDEN REALIZATION, INSPIRATION, AND INSIGHT FROM 26 PROFESSIONAL MEN

After spending more than four decades as a university professor and campus administrator, Dr. Newhouse made the decision to share his extensive expertise with others in the coaching realm. An exceptional listener who proceeds with his clients without judgment, he challenges his clients to let go of their apprehension and develop into the successful beings they were born to become. Dr. Newhouse is also extremely interested in conducting workshops, focus groups, and symposia on issues such as Tacit Knowledge, Surviving your Kids to Adulthood, Credence Goods, and Fathering Fatherless Boys.

Dr. Newhouse has received numerous awards, such as Who's Who in Black America, Who's Who in America, Who's Who in Canada, and Outstanding Young Men of America (twice), and Outstanding Teacher of America (twice). Dr. Newhouse is most grateful for the many tokens of love and appreciation he has received from 40 years of university teaching, including a plaque, certificates, mugs, and thank-you cards.

In addition to his successful career in teaching and coaching, Dr. Newhouse is an accomplished author, publishing eight books. These include *Hope, the Big Headed Cat* and *Holy Moly, a Book of Holes*. Dr. Newhouse has published four spiritual poem books, such as *By the Breath of His Mouth* and *Call Me Old Shoes*. Dr. Newhouse is currently working on two books: a book about **Be Flat**, that examines how to be frank, straight forward and honest in communicating with others and *Belly-to-Belly*, a series of children's books chronicling the interactive stories of six 5-year-olds to their adolescence and adulthood.

Dr. Newhouse's involvement with Emmanuel Christian Institute is as its Vice President for Institutional Advancement. In that role, Dr. Newhouse is responsible for grant writing and institutional development. Dr. Newhouse travels frequently to the US, with dual US and Canadian citizenship, and was instrumental in assisting President Welch in the day-to-day operations of the Institute and 2015 Minister's Breakfast, Silent Auction, and

Convocation. In 2016, Dr. Newhouse will be the keynote speaker for this event.

During his collegiate career, Dr. Newhouse earned a Bachelor of Arts in psychology from Marietta College, where he was a member of Beta Kappa Chi, Tau Epsilon Phi fraternity, and on the Dean's List. He also earned a Master of Science degree in general experimental psychology and a PhD in experimental social psychology from Howard University (1980). In addition, Dr. Newhouse completed courses toward a Master of Business Administration degree at Strayer University.

Dr. Newhouse is a deacon and member of the Group Meeting (Governing Board) of Temple Baptist Church in Montreal, Quebec. He is also the choirmaster and co-coordinator of the Men's Fellowship.

Dr. Newhouse was baptized at five years old with his now-deceased younger sister, Amanda, when she was three. He has been actively involved in church work throughout his life and is committed to the vision that God has given Dr. Welch for ECI.

Dr. Newhouse is married and lives in Montreal with his wife, a step-son, and a step-daughter. He also has an adult daughter, who lives in Virginia.

OF SUDDEN REALIZATION, INSPIRATION, AND INSIGHT FROM 26 PROFESSIONAL MEN

Your Burdens Become Your Blessings
Clint Boyd Jr.

I've had two significant A-ha Moments in my life. When I was sixteen years old, I was at a marching band competition in my hometown and noticed a college student leaning on a fence watching the bands play. He had on purple and gold fraternity paraphernalia from a well-known and respected fraternity. We never spoke to each other and he never said a word while I was there. There was just something about his demeanor that spoke volumes to me about his self-confidence, self-awareness, and self-assurance. I remember thinking, "Man, I want to become one of them."

A couple of years later, I was a freshman engineering student at the University of Tennessee on a four-year academic scholarship. I saw a poster announcing an interest meeting for those interested in gaining more knowledge about the fraternity that the guy from my hometown belonged to. I attended the meeting and found out that the Omega Psi Phi fraternity was founded in 1911 on the principles of manhood, scholarship, perseverance, and uplift. The fraternity was a service-oriented social organization and had hundreds of thousands of members worldwide, some of whom were famous. The fraternity also had the reputation for making it extremely difficult to become a member because the choice was made based on very tough physical and mental pledging activities. It was scary, but I was immediately intrigued. There was word that they were about to pledge a line of potential candidates (pledges). There were about 10 of us who came to the meeting to hear more about the fraternity.

One of the members stood up and announced, "Only two of y'all are going to make it." I looked around the room at the other potential candidates and made predictions in my mind: "Only two people, huh? Let me see...me and him; no, me and him; no, maybe me and him." I was just that determined from the onset.

Sure enough, I made line but there were four other guys who made line with me. Pledging was everything they had told us and then some. The requirements were so tough that my grades suffered tremendously. I became a member, and the next semester I partied with the brothers so much my grades suffered again. After two semesters of poor grades, I lost my academic scholarship. My parents were upset and my father took the three-hour bus ride from my hometown to my dorm room, took the keys to the car he had purchased for me, and drove it back home. I was angry, embarrassed and faced with having to improve my grades or be kicked out of the university.

It took a few semesters but I finally got things together and graduated with a BS in industrial engineering. Employers weren't exactly knocking on my door after graduation. My grades were average and my work experience, while in college, was from jobs totally unrelated to my field of study. I had spent the summers working for the university's housekeeping department stripping and waxing floors, painting dorm rooms, and moving furniture. I also was attending classes to try to get caught up and improve my GPA.

My first job offer after graduation was with the federal government earning several thousand dollars less than the average entry-level engineer was making at the time. I made the best out of it and gained a lot of knowledge and experience there. Three years later, I landed a good job with a major oil and gas company making a good salary. I was married and living in Houston, Texas. My parents came to visit my wife, Elaine, and me.

In a sidebar conversation, my mother revealed that my father was disappointed in me for allowing the fraternity to overshadow my academic achievement in college. My father had shared with

her his feelings that had I not pledged the fraternity I would have made better grades. If I had achieved better grades, in his mind, I would have received better job offers and made higher salaries. When I asked him about it, he confirmed what my mother told me. He said that since I had a full-ride academic scholarship, he had purchased the car he gave me as a high school graduation gift with the money that he had saved for me to attend college. When I lost my scholarship, they had to scrape the money together for me to complete my degree. He was not only disappointed in my performance, but also in the cavalier attitude I displayed about how it affected them financially.

Honestly, I hadn't even thought about it from that perspective. I was so happy to have realized the dream of becoming an Omega Man that I hadn't considered how it had affected them. But it was deeper than that. Making the fraternity against incredible odds was a rite of passage to manhood for me. I explained to both of them that pledging the fraternity was the most difficult thing I had ever encountered in the 18 years I had been on earth. Before then, everything came easy to me. I was both popular and smart in high school. I was the president of the student council and excelled at everything I put my mind to. Pledging the fraternity, and then subsequently being forced to dig deep and force myself to turn things around academically, was the first true test of what I was made of. Nothing I had experienced prior to that had fully prepared me to overcome the challenges I faced. It is said that there can be no testimony without a test. Finding the nerve and sinew to make the fraternity, and then to push through in the face of failing out of college, was the first true test of many I would face in the years to come.

It was good for my father and me to have that conversation. It changed the dynamic of our relationship from father-to-son to man-to-man. We both got to share how the event that had taken place years prior had affected each of us. He had seen it as all bad. I had seen it as all good. In the end, we could both relate to each other's circumstances. I was regretful for the financial burden it had placed on my parents. He saw how it was the catalyst of my becoming a man.

That was my first *A-ha Moment*. When I look back on my life now, I've noticed that it is the difficult times in life where we really grow, if we pay attention and learn from our mistakes. I often hear people say, "I am blessed, in spite of my problems." But really, we are blessed because of them. They present us with opportunities to grow, learn, and improve. They allow us to exercise our faith muscles. Once those muscles are exercised, they are stronger and make us better prepared for the next challenge we face. I know that the man I am, and the man I am becoming, is largely due to the suffering I've endured and the challenges I've overcome, with faith in God, and help from many others. Your burdens become your blessings.

I had much success and made lots of money during the years I spent in corporate America. I was trained well and was taught some serious skills. The experiences I had all those twenty-plus years, leading up to my decision to start my own business, prepared me for what I am doing now. But the work I am doing now is what I have been truly called to do.

When I was climbing the corporate ladder, I achieved a lot and received a lot of awards, mostly all related to production-related goals: top 5% in sales, gross profit awards, engineering excellence, etc. It was great to achieve success and be recognized for my accomplishments, but all of the awards, rewards, and recognition I received primarily benefited my family and me.

In 2005, Elaine and I decided to start Higher Ground Training Inc., a company that provides personal and professional development training for companies interested in enhancing the productivity of their people. We wanted to take everything we'd learned, from our successes and failures, and help others reach their highest potential—their next higher self.

OF SUDDEN REALIZATION, INSPIRATION, AND INSIGHT FROM 26 PROFESSIONAL MEN

The business didn't take off like a rocket, so we experienced many seasons of famine. We started our company from ground zero and faced an uphill climb for years. Much like my successes in high school hadn't prepared me for the challenges I faced in college, the successes we experienced in corporate America hadn't properly prepared us for the level and duration of suffering it would take to bring our vision to fruition. However, like my experience in college, it is because of the challenges we faced with the business that we have been made better people. Before we could teach others how to reach their higher selves, we had to reach our own. I always tell people, "If you really want to get to know God, start a business. You will get to know him really well. You will spend hours talking, praying, and pleading with him."

As engineers, my wife and I had always made really good money. Starting a business from the ground up was the first time we had been financially challenged. Because we had experienced what it was like to be without, we developed empathy for those who are without. Because we had less, we learned how to be more prudent with our finances. Because we couldn't do the things we used to do, we were humbled. Because others shared with us in our times of need, we developed a heart for sharing. Sharing is serving and we became great servants of others. Even when things were tough for us, we kept doing for others. Sometimes sharing is the only thing that can make a burdened heart feel good.

Now that God has brought abundance to our company, we are already in the spirit of giving and serving. Often the first question we ask ourselves upon getting a check from a client is, "Who do we know in need who we can bless?" Our two children, who have gone through the storm with us, have developed generous hearts as well. And that same spirit of giving resides in our business, as we have provided hundreds of thousands of dollars worth of pro-bono training and coaching services to the underserved and causes we believe in.

In the years since we have started our company, I have

achieved a lot and received a lot of awards, but lately the awards have been mostly character-related. These most recent awards include Tom Joyner's Real Fathers Real Men Award (for providing pro bono training services to inmates), Visionary Award (for helping ex-offenders successfully re-enter society and the workforce), Christian Manhood Award (for starting a home repair and restoration program for widows), Omega Man of the Year Award (for multiple service-related projects), Volunteer of the Decade Award (for 10 years of volunteer service at a maximum security institution).

My second *A-ha Moment* was when I realized that the true key to success is uncovering our purpose and our God-given gifts and using those gifts in the service of others. When we take the focus off of ourselves, we gain the power to positively affect the lives of others. That's when God smiles down on us and true abundance, in all things, flows our way.

> "Give, and it will be given to you. A good measure, pressed down, shaken together and running over, will be poured into your lap. For with the measure you use, it will be measured to you." (Luke 6:38)

OF SUDDEN REALIZATION, INSPIRATION, AND INSIGHT FROM 26 PROFESSIONAL MEN

Bio of Clint Boyd (deceased)

Clint Boyd Jr. is the co-owner of Higher Ground Training, Inc., a company that offers training courses focused on personal and professional development for companies interested in enhancing the productivity of their people.

Higher Ground's clients include Nissan North America, the Tennessee Titans, the Nashville Area Chamber of Commerce, the Tennessee Department of Human Resources, Vanderbilt University, Tennessee State University, Nashville Electric Service, Bridgestone Firestone Tire Company and the US Environmental Protection Agency.

Clint holds a BS in industrial engineering from the University of Tennessee, Knoxville. Prior to starting Higher Ground in 2005, he worked for twenty years in corporate America.

In addition to the training services provided to business professionals, Clint provides training to inmates and ex-offenders to help them develop their personal and professional skills and achieve success upon re-entry to society.

Clint serves as the Educational Committee Chair of the Minority Business Enterprise Input Committee for the TriState Minority Supplier Development Council (TMSDC), which represents the interest of nearly 400 certified minority business enterprises in Tennessee, Kentucky, and West Virginia. He is on the board of directors for Samaritan Ministries, a nonprofit entity that provides warm meals and clothing to the homeless in Nashville, Tennessee, six days per week. Clint is a member of the Omega Psi Phi fraternity, where he serves as chapter reporter for the Nashville graduate chapter. He is also an ordained deacon at the Temple Baptist Church in Nashville, Tennessee.

In 2009, Clint was named the Real Fathers Real Men Award recipient on the Tom Joyner Morning Show, a nationally syndicated radio program that reaches eight million listeners. The award recognized his volunteer efforts training inmates at Riverbend Maximum Security Institution in Nashville, Tennessee, to prepare them for successful re-entry into society and the workforce. In 2010, Clint received the Accomplished Alumni Award from the University of Tennessee, Knoxville. In 2011, Clint received the Omega Man of the Year Award from the Gamma Phi chapter of the Omega Psi Phi fraternity. In 2012, Clint received the Outstanding Service Award from the Riverbend Maximum Security Institution for conducting pro-bono training for inmates enrolled in a 30-week rehabilitation curriculum called *Project: New Beginning*. In 2013, Clint received the Representative Harold M. Love Visionary Award for equipping male and female ex-offenders with the necessary job-readiness skills to successfully re-enter society and the workforce. Later in 2013, Clint received the Outstanding Service Award, for the second consecutive year, from the Riverbend Maximum Security Institution. At the end of 2013, Clint received the Omega Man of the Year Award from the Gamma Phi chapter of the Omega Psi Phi fraternity. In 2014, Clint received both the 5th District (TN & KY) Graduate Omega Man of the Year Award and the Volunteer of the Decade Award from the Riverbend Maximum Security Institution's *Project: New*

Beginning.

Clint lives in Hendersonville, Tennessee, with his wife and business partner, Elaine, his daughter, Jordan, and his son, Winston.

Looking Back
Wilbert Haywood Grandy Sr.

Transcript from Wilbert Haywood Grandy Sr.
Taken May 24, 2014

(At 92 years old, Mr. Grandy dictated into the editor's iPhone because he had not used his tape recorder in a long time.)

I guess my growing up was quite different from a lot of people, because I grew up on a farm. My father and my mother separated when I was quite young, and my grandmother raised me. I spent most of my time with my grandmother and my grandmother's sister, which is my aunt. They ran a small farm, they called in those days "sharecroppers" in Wilson Mills, North Carolina. In a sharecropper's farm, there are white persons who owned the land, and they would let you tend part of the land for the produce that you produce. That's the way I kind of grew up. I learned how to plow, to pick cotton, and stuff like that.

Through my growing up days, I was a very competitive person. When it came to picking cotton, I always could pick more than the average person my age. There was one handicap there and being on a farm, at least it was with me.

When schools opened, I couldn't go until about October, because I couldn't go to school until the cotton was picked. But

OF SUDDEN REALIZATION, INSPIRATION, AND INSIGHT FROM 26 PROFESSIONAL MEN

what happened by December, or later on in the year, I was ahead of the class because I was very competitive and each grade that I passed I was the top person in the class all the time. And one of my best subjects was mathematics. I knew my math. So when I graduated from high school, I was told that I was the second highest person in the class, but years later when I went back to Wilson Mills, I met some of my former teachers, and they told me, "You were number one in the class! The reason you were second, the principal of the school didn't want you to be first," and he said, "I knew what I was talking about because I was the one who manipulated your grade, so you'd be second." So we laughed about it. That's made no difference because I had finished college now. But what happened when I finished high school, my father told me that he could pay my tuition for one year and after that "you are going to have to go for yourself." I said okay. So I chose A & T College in North Carolina and my major I chose was mathematics. So at the end of that first year at A & T, I was the head of my class because of the "competitive in me". At the time, my father was living in Raleigh, and my mother at the time was living in Washington, DC. So I stayed in close contact with each one of them.

My mother told me, "You can go to Howard University if you want to and come up to stay with me. You can get a job and there is a good chance you can go to Howard."

I said, "Well, I think I'd rather be a Howard graduate." So at the end of the first year, I came to live with my mother and I got a job working with a delivery company, a freight delivery company. So I finished high school at 19. One year later I finished North Carolina AT College, and during the summer I was in Washington, DC with my mother and I was getting a job with the freight company, unloading the freight cars.

At the time, most of the merchandise was moved by freight trucks. So I did pretty good because I had to work hard and freight is a noisy job. I made it alright and I got promoted during the summer. They promoted me to a checker/cashier. So all I had to do was

[take] a pad and a pencil and write down numbers as the other guys unloaded the cars. Each freight package has a number on it. They called out numbers and I wrote it down. By the end of the summer I was a truck driver. Truck drivers made more money than anybody else. So I did that until late that year.

I went to Howard University for one full semester and the Army called me. So I chose the Army. I had a chance to select what unit I wanted to be in. My first job was to go out on the mountain and we had a sledge hammer, cracked these rocks , put them in a barrel and rolled them in the truck and the truck was bringing them to a crusher where we got that quite large rock. So I told the sergeant, "Look at my hands, I've never done kind of work like this. Don't you have an office job?" Then he asked me, "Can you type?" I said, "Sure. I can type 75 words a minute." That was a little exaggerated, but sure. He said, "I got that kind of position for you." So a few days later, he told me to go to the office. I went there and I typed maybe 40 words per minute or so.

I practiced. I got better for the organization and typed whatever needed to be typed. There wasn't long before I got promoted. In one year, I moved from private staff sergeant to head of the personnel office. I got a lot of comments about the way I handled personnel. So at the end of two years, I took the examination for officer training school and I passed the examination, but I did not get the officer training school. I had some problems with my stomach, so they decided to give me an honorable discharge. So I got my discharge, came back, and started back working at the freight yard again. When the fall came around again, I was able to get back into Howard University. This time I was able to get enough GI benefits to go to the school in pharmacy. I finished pharmacy school at the top of my class in 1949. So from then on, I started to get jobs as a pharmacist. I worked at one store for a while and met a physician who wanted to set up a clinic. He was a very popular guy. We became friends. He set it up, and I was the pharmacist owner of a pharmacy within that clinic.

After a year, I had some disagreement with the owner of that clinic and decided to move to another location. I moved there and rented a store for a couple of years until business began to get slow. What happened was that they were building more pharmacies and they were experiencing more customers and prosperity than smaller businesses.

The larger pharmacies began to put out more stores and put the smaller drug stores out of business because of the low prices. I sold my drug store to another drug store owner who had a professional pharmacy. I worked together with him for about 6 years and then he sold the store to another pharmacist named Gibson.

Gibson and I were together at professional pharmacy for 10 years until one day the police found his body dead. His wife took over his store because I did not want it.

I worked as a manager for a professional pharmacist with her for a few years until I was offered a job in the DC government. I went to a local department of Human Resources and I operated the clinic for the District of Columbia.

When I decided to retire, I invited all the pharmacists' assistants that had worked with me to give them a lunch. When I told my supervisor what my idea was, she said "Oh! That is a wonderful idea!" She said that hadn't been done before. I said I was going to do something for all of them who had been helpful to me.

I decided that as I was retiring from this position, I just want to show them my appreciation. One member of the pharmacy, the public health officer, gave me the access to the facility. So I gave a luncheon for 20 people. One other pharmacy said, "so, Grandy, did you pay for the whole thing by yourself?" I said "Sure!" He said "No, I am already getting ready to retire myself, I will help you out." I said "Okay, I'll pay half and you'll pay half of it." So the two of us gave the big luncheon and then afterward the supervisor decided to give me a retirement party. She said, "No other pharmacists had had a retirement party, so you are going to be the first one. We are going to give you one (in 2001)."

In my 93 years of life, I have experienced many *A-ha Moments*. To recount a few, the first thing you want to do is make yourself a representative for the people around you, your contact people. Be an example for somebody, especially young people, which means take what jobs you can get, any job you can get, and do your best on that job so that you don't have to stay in the position you first selected and move up the ladder. So, that is what I have done throughout my lifetime, starting low and working up, and I was able to do this by people who worked with me, or around me, or people I worked for, saw that I was aggressive and said "you can handle a better job" in whatever position I had.

If things are not good for you, work it out. It might not be to your satisfaction what you are doing, until you can do something better. Most people these days want to start at the top, but that's not always the best place to start. Start wherever you are able to start, and prove yourself there, because the experience you get when you are starting at the bottom will help you when you get to the top. I was born July 5, 1920, and my next birthday I will be **94 years old**.

One thing, many times when you move up, you are going to have to move back. A lot of things are going to happen as you work your way up. Everything is not going to be easy, and you are going to be fired from a good job, you are going to have to take a job you don't like, but whatever the situation is, work it out.

I always heard "one step back, two steps forward," and that's the way to go. Don't give up when things don't go right. Tomorrow is going to be a better day.

Bio of Wilbert Haywood Grandy, Sr.

After he finished at Howard University's School of Pharmacy in 1949 with a BS degree in pharmacy, employment for black pharmacists was quite limited. They could only work in a black pharmacy because the white stores would not hire black people, so his idea was to start his own business. Eventually, in 1958, he was able to get a little money and start a private pharmacy on his own. His drug store specialized basically in just filling prescriptions. He had a pretty good business for about 10 years, and the other stores began to hire black pharmacists. His business, which primarily specialized in filling prescriptions, began to shrink, and eventually he went out of business.

Mr. Grandy then became a manager at a local store. He served as a manager of a black store for quite a few years, until 1990, when the black store business as such began to fade away and did not have quite an impact on the community anymore, because people could go to any drugstore they wanted to go. He then started working for the District of Columbia as a pharmacist in the neighborhood clinic. That gives you a summary of part of his history.

When Mr. Grandy started working for the government, he started taking extra courses in health care and did it to improve his status in the clinic, by being able to provide additional health care to members who would come into the clinic. His knowledge of pharmacy increased to the point that the doctors who worked in the clinic began to call him and rely upon him to facilitate in them treating their patients. They would say such things as "What would you recommend if a patient had a certain illness, and what certain drugs might the patient be able to take?" and "What would you prescribe to patients that would not conflict with other medications the patient was taking?"

He got a strong reputation with the people he worked with in the clinic. He retired at the age of 80, and had built up such a reputation among the clinics that they hated to see him go. They gave him a big retirement party. In addition, upon retiring from the Department of Human Services, Commission on Mental Health Services, Mr. Grandy received a Letter of Thanks from the mayor of Washington, a Meritorious Service Award from the DC government and a letter dated May 29, 2001, from the White House and President George Bush.

Since the 1970s, Mr. Grandy also has taken additional courses in the School of Religion at Howard University and served as a Sunday School teacher until five years ago.

At 93, Mr. Grandy does not do any extra work in the community. In his own words, "I have not volunteered for anything. When I retired, I completely retired."

OF SUDDEN REALIZATION, INSPIRATION, AND INSIGHT FROM 26 PROFESSIONAL MEN

From Electronics to Evangelism
Pastor Joseph Hovsepian

The Early Years

I am the son of two survivors of the Armenian genocide, which started in 1915 in Turkey and in which, by the end of 1920, 1.5 million Armenians were massacred, including both my grandfathers. My grandmothers survived and ran toward the sea to save their lives.

My maternal grandmother was pregnant with my uncle (Stepan). My mother was about five years old, and even though people encouraged my grandmother to leave her little daughter behind and save herself, she said: "Never! Either we will both survive or both be killed." Thankfully, a Greek boat rescued them and brought them to Greece. (This story can actually fill a book, but that's for another time.)

Nearly two decades later, I was born in Athens. It was around the time World War II started (1939). My parents were refugees and very poor. Daily, people were dying in the streets of hunger and diseases. In 1945, WWII ended, but a civil war started, which went on for about three years.

As a child, I became fascinated by war machines and equipment; anything mechanical or electrical fascinated me. I am not sure what made me develop a great interest in experiments and technology. Was it the war activities, or was it my endless desire to reach out into the vastness of space and its numberless stars, wondering about infinity and eternity until my palms got sweaty and my heart raced?

My first *A-ha Moment* came when I, as usual, was investigating my father's motorcycle, wanting to know how it got its initial power. I took a long nail and put it across the battery's poles marked + and − and the nail started to glow. It continued to glow and finally melted. I knew then that I wanted to be an electrician. Experimenting and building things led me to choose electronics and electro-mechanics for my future. I studied for a year and then joined the Royal Greek Air Force, where I served as an aircraft wireless engineer.

While serving in the Air Force, I decided to emigrate to Canada. My application eventually was approved and I received my papers; unfortunately, the final date to enter Canada was about two months before the date I was going to finish my Air Force duties. I was devastated. I thought those two months would keep me from going to Canada.

After trying everything I could to change these arrangements, and failing, I said, "I will go directly to the highest authority in the land: the queen of Greece." I wrote a very passionate letter to her, presenting my predicament. I also prayed that God would touch her heart. A few weeks later, having read my letter, the queen instructed the Air Force authorities to give me an honourable discharge.

I arrived in Canada on April 13. Two days later, I started work as an electrician in the construction industry for $1.00 an hour. A friend asked, "Why don't you apply for a job at Canadair [later renamed Bombardier]?" I could hardly speak English and knew no French, but I applied anyway.

A few days later, I was offered the position of a troubleshooter in the pre-flight department. After working there for about two years, I started my own business called "Radio Hovsep Electronics," which I still have and operate today.

My Faith

I was born into a Christian (evangelical) family and, from

childhood, I was taught Christian biblical values and principles. Going to church was part of my life and very natural. At the age of 12, I stood up during a New Year's Eve service and dedicated my life to God and his service.

About three years later, my father called and said: "Son, I want to talk with you." I thought, *He is going to talk to me about girls and sex*. But I was wrong. He said: "Son, I want you to become a pastor, so I will get an extra job to help you study in a Swiss school, but if you want to continue with your desire to be an electrician, then I will pray for you." I responded: "Father, please pray for me; I don't want to be a pastor." I never left the church or my faith, but I did excel in business and electronics.

In 1970, several years after my marriage, I traveled around the world for over a month and visited Asian, Middle Eastern, and European countries. I saw all kinds of religious temples and churches, observing their traditions and belief systems, trying to find the truth about religion.

On my way back home, I came to the conclusion that all man-made religions had some good, some hope to offer, but not the whole truth as I wanted to find and believe. It was at that stage of my life that the next and most important *A-ha Moment* came for me. I understood that all man-made religions resembled empires or businesses. So I rejected religion and dedicated my life and service to the living God and creator. Jesus Christ was now my living hope and my life. From then on, I continued serving in the church with a new focus and mission.

It was in early 1984 that our church members asked me to become the pastor. After my wife and friends encouraged me, I accepted the role and went through the necessary examination process to be ordained. I still serve there as the pastor today.

After about thirty years of serving as a volunteer pastor, I had one more *A-ha Moment*. In 2008, my wife was getting ready to attend a school reunion in Armenia (she was actually born in

Egypt and had never been to Armenia before). While praying and meditating, I believe I was inspired by God to join my wife in Armenia, on the condition that I would go to the villages and visit the poor and forgotten people of that land. This would be my first visit, too.

It quickly became very clear that these people had great needs and I knew that, with God's help, I could support them. I did what I could then and promised to return with more help. They needed money for medication, clothing, food, housing, etc., but their emotional and spiritual needs were greater and these were ignored by the affluent world.

I decided to start a mission group and called it Joseph Hovsepian Ministries. My wife, my two daughters, a young lady in Armenia, and I are the official members of this ministry, but there are many who have been helping and supporting us to continue.

In August 2014, my daughter Ann-Margret and I will be going back to Armenia; it will be her second visit and my fifth. We have printed and distributed more than two million pamphlets and 10,000 books, and bought and distributed more than 1,000 Bibles to help meet spiritual needs. We have also given large amounts of money to help with medical bills, medication, the renovation of a church building, and transportation expenses for the workers there.

Now, at the age of 75, I am not sure whether any more *A-ha Moments* will come before my great A-HA MOMENT in heaven.

of Sudden Realization, Inspiration, and Insight from 26 Professional Men

Bio of Joseph Hovsepian

Joseph Hovsepian was born in Athens, Greece, in 1939 and emigrated to Montreal, Canada, in 1960. He is both a full-time volunteer pastor of a Baptist church and the owner of Radio Hovsep Electronics, a unique shop where he sells and repairs new and antique radios and other electronics.

` Although he is well past retirement age, Hovsepian, who speaks five languages, continues to enjoy operating his business. His greatest passion, however, is sharing the love of Jesus with those he meets, whether at work, at church, in his neighborhood, or in another part of the world.

When I Look in the Mirror
Bruce A. Herman

My father was a member of what Tom Brokaw called "The Greatest Generation." I certainly can't argue with that moniker, as these men following the Great Depression went off to fight a war against Nazi Germany and Imperialist Japan. To me, however, my father was distant and aloof, taking very little interest in me during my formative years. I remember when he gave me my first baseball mitt and we went out into the driveway to have a catch. I must have been about 5 or 6 years old, but I thought of this as a real father-and-son moment. When my father gave me the mitt, he placed it on my left hand, put the ball in my right hand, stepped back a few paces, and told me to throw it to him. I raised the ball over my head, reared back, like I had seen other ball players do at Maplecrest Park, and I let it go. The ball sailed high and wide, slipping out of my hand, coming to rest far from my father, who was no more than five or six feet away.

The very act of throwing the ball felt strange and awkward. We tried it a few more times with very little success. Even at such a young age, I knew that something was wrong. My father came over to me, took the glove off my left hand, and told me to put it on my right hand. Following his instructions, I took the glove and put my thumb in the spot where your pinky goes and filled the other finger holes accordingly. I put the ball in my left hand and tried to throw it back to my father once again. This time, the act of throwing felt more natural and I was able to make the ball go right back to my father, avoiding another embarrassingly high and errant throw. We did this a few times, and he came over to me and said, "I guess you're a lefty and we need to get you another glove." At the time I thought, "Wow, my dad discovered that I was a lefty," and how smart he must be to figure this out. Many years later, after we had our first child, it dawned on me as to how out of touch my father was with his children, not realizing that his son was a lefty until the boy was six years old.

During my grammar, junior high, and high school years, my father rarely attended any of my wrestling matches, baseball games, or lacrosse games. He always reminded me that he was my father and didn't want to become my friend as he saw other parents do to their kids. I accepted this concept and felt how lucky I was that my dad wanted to play his role as father and not try to be a friend. I honestly thought that other kids and their dads were making a mistake by becoming friends by going to sporting events together, watching their kids' athletic practices, and being more involved in their lives. Growing up in the 50s and early 60s, some of my other friends' fathers were much like my dad, remaining at least an arm's length distance from their sons while other friends' dads were just the opposite, taking an active interest in their development.

At the end of my freshman year in high school, my parents moved our family about an hour south from northern to central New Jersey (exit 9 off the turnpike), where my father (with a partner) started a small employment agency. The move was difficult for me, but I did manage to make a few new friends during my high school years.

A few years later, I was accepted at a small liberal arts college in southeastern Ohio and fell in love with the school, the small town of Marietta, and its rural surroundings. It was so different from my urban upbringing in northern New Jersey. I made a lot of friends at college and thought life would be smooth sailing the rest of the way. At the time, the deal I had with my parents was that they would pay for room, board, and tuition. I was responsible for all other expenses. I had a great time and was elected freshman class president, joined a fraternity, made the Dean's List both semesters, and balanced my academic life with my social life very well.

When I got home following my freshman year, my parents informed me that if I wanted to go back to school, I would need to take out a college loan, apply for a scholarship, and be prepared to pay for all my expenses. I did all of that, and worked two jobs over the summers and during school vacations. I also worked at the fraternity house in order to get my dues paid and picked up odd jobs on campus so that I could have a few extra bucks of spending money while at school. Of course, going to college in the late 60s and early 70s made it rather easy to live on next to nothing. All one needed was a few pairs of jeans, a few work shirts, a few candles, some furniture from Goodwill, some rolling papers, and a bit of intellectual curiosity. It was a great time to be a college student. For a better understanding of my psyche and those of other students in college during the late 60s and early 70s, our "bible" was a book that became a best seller called <u>Greening of America</u> by Charles Reich. As a matter of fact, we spent the entire first semester of my political science class that year discussing it cover to cover.

I finished my four years of college, fell in love with a beautiful woman I had met when we were both freshmen, got married shortly after graduation, and entered the business world. I got an entry-level job in the wine business in New Jersey, of all places, and began to learn how to sell and merchandise wine. I suppose you could say that I was very ambitious and worked as many hours as were necessary to get the job done. Even though I was a history major in college, once I landed a job in the wine industry, I wanted to learn as much as possible about both the history and the business of wine. In a short period of time, I gained a reputation among my managers, my peers, and my supervisor for being reliable and a potential "rising star" in the company.

I won't bore you with the details of my resume, but I have

OF SUDDEN REALIZATION, INSPIRATION, AND INSIGHT FROM 26 PROFESSIONAL MEN

worked for some of the best companies in the wine and spirits industry, including Diageo and Moet Hennessy, representing some of the greatest beverage alcohol brands like Johnnie Walker, Tanqueray, Moet Champagne, and Beringer Wines. I'm proud of my career, the contacts I've made, and the things that I've accomplished in the business world. I have been given many wonderful experiences, like the time we flew from New York to Paris on the Concorde to celebrate Moet Champagne's 250th Anniversary at the Palace of Versailles. We had a private tour of the palace and attended a private dinner for 150 of "your closest friends" on the grounds of the Palace of Versailles. It was surely a once-in-a-lifetime experience.

Below the surface, contributing to my success was my fear of financial failure. I was fearful of not having the ability to build a secure financial environment for my wife and our children. In short, I was always running scared and concerned that I would end up like my father, not being able to send my kids to college or to help them out as they moved through their lives. So as a result, I worked very hard at becoming a student of my chosen profession. An *A-ha Moment* for me was that hard work and long hours focused on your profession does pay off.

Another *A-ha Moment* was when I transferred the knowledge I gained through my schooling into a successful business. Learning from each of my experiences and always applying those lessons to my current and projected future situations contributed to growing my capabilities, enhancing my reputation as a leader in my chosen industry, and developing a successful career.

We moved coast to coast three times; I rarely took vacations more than a long weekend, and generally worked six days a week to get the job done. I had (and still have) a very understanding, caring, supportive, and self-sustaining wife. Just prior to what became our last cross-country transfer from New York to San Francisco, my wife told me that if we were to make this move, it came with a few conditions. First of all, the job had better pay pretty well because she wasn't planning on going back to work. Secondly, I needed to move the office from Los Angeles to San Francisco because she wasn't going to live in southern California. Finally, the company had better gross up the moving expenses because we learned that the IRS considers it additional income and our prior moves resulted in us paying more than our fair share of income taxes on moving/living expenses. I went back to the president of the company, who had initiated the discussion about my running the Western states, and he agreed to our conditions.

In 1986, we moved from northern New Jersey to Marin County in northern California and began to lay down our roots in the community. Two years later, our oldest son, David, age 6, got a younger brother, Matthew. David became very involved in sports with a focus on swimming and water polo. His younger brother Matthew followed in his footsteps and in spite of (or maybe because of) their age difference, they have become the best of friends.

As you can imagine, I continued to work like a maniac, traveling extensively and building the Western region into one of the top business units for the company. I did, however, know that my kids were right-handed. I bought them the correct baseball gloves and I attended as many swimming and water polo meets as possible. My kids also knew that I was their father as well as their friend when they needed or wanted me to be in that role. The following examples seem to show how my kids understood me and my role as their father.

When David and Jessica got married last summer, they asked us to officiate at their wedding, which was quite a thrill and very special. David and I play golf together on a regular basis and enjoy each other's company. Matthew, following his graduation from UC San Diego, entered the wine business two years ago. We speak almost daily about his activities, and he seeks my advice on his career development and how he can impact the business in his current role of managing sales for a top-notch spirits company in southern California. I'm very proud of him, as I am of his older brother, David, and absolutely thrilled that he decided, on his own, to enter the same profession as his dad.

With tremendous support from my wife and kids, I managed to earn an MBA in strategic leadership from Dominican University. The program required two full years of Saturday classes with a cohort group. Getting an MBA gave me the confidence to start two new businesses from scratch in the wine and spirits industry.

After I rebuilt the team and the business for the company that had moved me to California, I was tapped to become the Senior VP of Sales reporting to a newly appointed company president. Since the company's headquarters was in Manhattan, another cross-country move was required. At the time, our oldest son, David, was about to enter his junior year in high school and his favorite sport was water polo. Water polo is a very popular high school sport in the public schools in California, but not so in the Northeast, where it's big in private high schools, but not in public high schools. Neither my wife nor I wanted to pull our son out of his California high school and set him up in a new school without a water polo team. I remembered back to the time my folks moved the family from northern to central New Jersey and how I felt about that move. I therefore didn't want to do the same thing to my son that my parents did to me. This was another *A-ha Moment*, best described as remembering how situations affected you and trying your best not to repeat the same mistakes with those close to you.

My solution to not pulling David out of high school was that I commuted coast to coast for almost two years so that he could stay in his California high school. The plan was to move back to the East Coast when David graduated and went off to college. His brother, Matthew, would be going from grammar to middle school and therefore we planned to move at these two simultaneous transition points in our kids' lives.

During the middle of David's senior year in high school, my wife came to me and told me that neither she nor our kids wanted to move back to the East Coast. So there I was, a guy who has climbed the corporate ladder, having finally achieved one of the top

3–5 senior sales positions in the wine and spirits industry, and my family didn't want to make a move to the East Coast. What do I do? Force my wife and kids to move, believing that they will eventually adjust? Decide to have a trial separation followed by a divorce so that I could continue in this great job? Or turn this situation into an opportunity to change jobs and find something that could work for us and forgo the move? The industry is very small, so just the act of looking brought the risk of termination if my boss found out.

As you can imagine, many thoughts rolled through my mind. Then I had my *A-ha Moment* when I looked in the mirror and saw not only me, but most importantly my family. It became very clear to me that whatever my decision making process would be, I needed to prioritize my wife and my children's needs before my own. Becoming a "man" isn't about who you are as an individual. It's about how you treat those around you. Becoming a "man" is not really about you, it's all about them! It's about balancing your own needs with the needs of your loved ones. When someone becomes a "man," he should be most satisfied when those he loves find happiness through his conscious and deliberate acts of selflessness. So the next time you look in the mirror and see others before you see yourself, you will be on your way to becoming a man in the truest sense of the word.

Bio of Bruce A. Herman

Bruce A. Herman is the President of Independent Distillers North America and joined the New Zealand-based company in 2009. He is responsible for the marketing, sales, operations, and financial results of the company in the USA and Canada. Independent Liquor was founded in the mid-eighties in New Zealand, and has other operations in Australia. Bruce initially consulted for the company five years ago when it was owned by private equity. Having written a business plan to establish the company in the US, Bruce was asked to become its president and was charged with the responsibility of establishing a footprint in the US market while managing the Canadian operation. In October 2011, the company was sold to Asahi and Bruce remained as its North American president.

Prior to working with Independent Distillers, Bruce established a consulting business that focused on sales, distribution, and marketing in the wine and spirits industry. Bruce made the most of his extensive experience in sales, distribution, and route-to-market analysis. He believes in a pragmatic approach to marketing wines and spirits from a perspective of the supplier as well as the distributor. His consulting business provided focused and practical approaches to solving problems in the area of sales, distribution, and marketing in the wines and spirits industry.

Bruce Herman joined Foster's Wine Estates (then Beringer Blass Wine Estates and currently known as Treasury Wine Estates) in the position of Senior Vice President, Sales & Marketing, for North America in July 2004. His responsibility encompassed managing all sales and marketing activities for the US and Canada. Following the June 2005 acquisition of Southcorp Wines, Bruce became Senior Vice President, Sales, and led the integration of the two US and Canadian sales forces under the Foster's Wine Estates company reporting to Australia.

In his previous role as Senior Vice President and General Manager of The Estates Group, a semi-independent wholesale, sales, and marketing company he established in 1999 for California-based wholesaler Young's Market Company LLC, Bruce oversaw the distribution of such well-known brands as The Hess Collection Winery, Cakebread Cellars, and Schramsberg Vineyards throughout California.

Prior to that, Bruce was Senior Vice President of Sales for Schieffelin & Somerset Company, a joint-venture sales and marketing company owned by Moet Hennessy and Diageo, based in New York City. Bruce spent fourteen years with Schieffelin & Somerset, with the responsibility for brands such as Johnny Walker Scotch and Moet Champagne, in a series of positions, including National Sales Manager for California Wines and Western Zone Vice President.

Bruce began his career in 1973 as a merchandiser for United Vintners. Following United Vintners, he joined Mirassou Vineyards where he spent eight years, the last three as National Sales Manager.

"I think the wine business is very dynamic and interesting because it's always changing," commented Bruce. "And wine is a product that you can sell and market, but also enjoy on a personal level."

Bruce lives in Marin County, California, with his wife, Susan. They have two sons, David and Matthew.

Bruce holds a BA degree in history from Marietta College in Ohio and a MBA from the Dominican University of California.

Contact Information:

Bruce.herman01@gmail.com

A-ha Moments
Andreas Deligeorge

I was recently asked how I went from being an unpopular, scrawny, first-generation Canadian kid—one that other kids would throw dodge balls at and ridicule—to becoming a physically fit, self-made, work-from-home entrepreneur heading a cutting-edge online marketing company and earning a net six-figure income by age 30.

Simply put, I used the resources that were available to me, didn't give up when facing obstacles, made strategic decisions, and surrounded myself with the right people. In life, we have experiences. Each experience comes with a takeaway. Some experiences are negative—we often refer to such experiences as challenges, obstacles, or threats. Sometimes we can't control what happens in life. We can only control how we react.

Family Matters

I have to say that I am privileged to have been born and raised by my great family here in Canada, despite the long winters. My parents are happily married, and I benefited from the love of my entire family including my brother, my aunt and uncle, and my grandparents on both sides of my family. Having a sibling is great because it teaches you how to share and how to get along with others. Despite going through some relatively standard adolescent challenges, including being made fun of due to a big nose and oversized ears (acquiring nicknames along the way, including

Dumbo, Assman, and Andranus), I also faced the challenge of being the youngest student in my class, and at an earlier age, this can make school slightly more challenging. But that didn't stop me from winning the math award in my senior year of high school or graduating with honors in University.

Throughout my childhood, my parents, a fine-art instructor and a stay-at-home mom and piano teacher (who recently began a career in journalism), although they are fantastic, were quite stringent when it came to the integration and use of technology in our household. As a result, I was always the last kid to get my hands on new technology, including video games, a computer, an internet connection, and a mobile phone. In fact, to this day, my father, who recently turned sixty years old, does not have a cell phone or an email account. That didn't stop me from heading my own online marketing company.

That said, I was fortunate enough to have been allowed to live with my parents until I completed University. It is important to take advantage of everything and not to take anything for granted. For instance, I managed to acquire experience working in the fields of e-learning, design, online payment processing, affiliate marketing, and SEO (search engine optimization) throughout my studies. This helped me save money, build my skill set and my understanding of online-related technologies and industries, and apply many things I had learned in school.

Be Yourself

Following the completion of my school training, which specialized in math and science, I realized that I had no interest in becoming a doctor, lawyer, or engineer like my family would have strongly preferred at the time. In fact, even at a young age, my grandmother asked me what I wanted to be when I grow up, and I said "rich." I remember wanting to explore the theatre department when visiting an open house at a local college, and my grandmother refused to let me even go and check it out. Finally, I wound up getting a degree in illustration and design from Dawson College. It had some technological elements that appealed to me, such as the use and creative application of software, but it was also extremely creative and seemed very enjoyable, although challenging, to develop such a skill set.

Upon completion of this program of study, my recommendation letter from Lucy Trahan, the head of the department, read that I had a strong interest in entrepreneurship. Boy, was she on to something! I followed that degree up with a BA in communications and marketing from Concordia University, during which time I worked approximately 25–30 hours per week at an e-learning company, was a teaching assistant for courses in television aesthetics and Microsoft Office, and registered my own company: Omnivision Design.

Perhaps a few entrepreneurs reading this can relate to what I will say next: "The day I registered my company was the day I became a father." Becoming self-employed is a real responsibility, especially for someone new in the game. Not only that, but investing your time, money, and energy into such an initiative can be quite demanding, especially for a full-time student. I began taking baby steps and freelancing. I would complete all kinds of work and would handle all the production myself—I would complete flyer designs, business cards, CD covers, and various other projects myself—until one day I encountered a project that required food photography, which I was not proficient in. That was the first time I subcontracted work to another individual successfully.

Set SMART Objectives—How to Set Your Goals

The definition of "success" is to achieve one's goals. Therefore, what you need in order to be successful is to set objectives in place. Some individuals don't set any objectives, and then they wonder why they feel like they are in a slump or aren't inching their way toward their ideal lifestyle, career path, relationship, or success. Your objectives must be SMART (Specific, Measurable,

Achievable, Realistic, and Time-specific).

Surround Yourself with the Right People

You can't control who your family members are and whether they are positive or negative forces; if you are an employee, perhaps you have little control over who your colleagues are. However, you can certainly become conscious of and avoid the influence of family members and colleagues who are negative. Choose your friends, lovers, and business partners wisely and surround yourself with good, positive people who build you up, make you feel good about yourself, believe in you, are open-minded, and support your objectives. Networking events, online interactions, social media, and hosting interns have all played a big role in meeting the right people who I can collaborate with. As a general rule, you should be open-minded and give everyone a chance, but that said, always listen to your gut, and take measures to protect yourself if you perceive any potential risk, because mistakes and betrayals can happen in life. Throughout my years in business, some of my subcontractors have gone over my head and began to work directly with my clients. I have also had a salesperson, someone who had done a couple of months of work for me as an independent consultant, make false claims, stating that he was a full-time employee and that I owed him thousands of dollars. It is important to be able to react appropriately to such situations and move on.

Timing is Everything

My former business partner and project manager, who was a good friend of mine, urged me to take on a full-time employee earlier than I was prepared to. At the time, we were experiencing difficulty when outsourcing certain projects, but he eventually wound up leaving the company for personal reasons. Just over a year later, I had hired my first employee, a former intern who I had initially, reluctantly, taken on as an in-house web developer. When making the decision to hire him full time, I was definitely taking a risk because initially I didn't have enough projects to keep him busy. I requested that he upgrade our existing websites. This recent graduate seeking employment turned out to be the best, fastest, and most reliable developer I had ever encountered, despite his initial lack of experience. He is proactive, a hard worker, a great problem solver, and just celebrated his first-year anniversary at Omnivision Design. As a result, my company is capable of taking on a higher volume of web-development-related mandates, our prices remain competitive, and we are acquiring more requests from these clients for other services. These happy clients also tend to refer other new customers to us. Revenues have never been better.

Re-evaluate Your Definition of the Word Risk

Some people refrain from investing themselves in building a path towards achieving their objectives, principally out of insecurity and fear of failure. Many individuals fear change, others fear rejection; whatever the case may be, there are many potential-filled individuals who decide not to chase their dreams, reach for the stars, or think big. Regardless of your reasoning, if you are not making a decision to attempt change in your life and you do not strive to achieve your objectives, it's worse than taking a risk because it pretty much guarantees that you will not achieve your objectives (there is no possibility of failure, but there is no possibility of success). Set a goal. Take action.

Furthermore, I am a huge advocate of entrepreneurship and view risk much differently than most people. My perception of having a "secure job" is similar to investing in a single stock rather than diversifying your portfolio, or putting all your eggs in one basket. I believe it is better to have many different eggs and to put them into different baskets. If I lose one of my 100+ clients, it is not a good thing, but it isn't the end of the world either. On the other hand, if you lose your job, then what happens? So what is riskier? Being self-employed and serving multiple clients, or having a single employer and a single source of revenue? Furthermore, there are tax-saving possibilities when running your own business. Lucky for me, this whole conundrum was a no-brainer for me at an early stage of the game. That said, there is a plus and a minus to everything. It's just a question of your outlook and your priorities. Think positively, and take action toward your objectives.

As a friend and colleague of mine put it:

"It seems almost impossible to be unsuccessful here in North America – there are so many opportunities. If you are unsuccessful, you're probably doing something wrong."

Choose the Path That Will Help You Achieve Success

Throughout the years, as people age and experience life, they react differently to their surroundings and take one of two different paths: they either let themselves become manipulated by their surroundings—the words and actions of others—while others are resilient and acknowledge their current state, with their own strengths and weaknesses, and set proper objectives for themselves. Those people have a much better chance of achieving success.

Think Like a Kid: Be Fearless and Creative

Children are, in fact, much better at having a positive frame of mind due to their lack of negative experiences, including failure, rejection, injury, and such things. Children are naturally creative, often seemingly fearless, and do not truly understand that some actions yield certain consequences.

Do You Feel Lucky?

Whenever I am asked by a friend, relative, client or

colleague how I achieved such a successful life, I've tried saying that I got lucky, but each time I do so, I stand corrected by someone that has been close to me throughout the years. Here are a few sayings regarding luck that I wish to share with you, as I think they are quite important because it's too easy to look at successful people and think that their success was somehow a result of luck itself.

"Inspiration is one thing and you can't control it, but hard work is what keeps the ship moving. Good luck means, work hard. Keep up the good work." – Kevin Eubanks

"My success was due to good luck, hard work, and support and advice from friends and mentors. But most importantly, it depended on me to keep trying after I had failed." – Mark Warner

"Shallow men believe in luck. Strong men believe in cause and effect." – Ralph Waldo Emerson

"I've found that luck is quite predictable. If you want more luck, take more chances. Be more active. Show up more often." – Brian Tracy

"Diligence is the mother of good luck." – Benjamin Franklin

"People often remark that I'm pretty lucky. Luck is only important in so far as getting the chance to sell yourself at the right moment. After that, you've got to have talent and know how to use it." – Frank Sinatra

    I think you get the idea here. Essentially, the definition of luck in my book is consistently and persistently working toward your goals and overcoming obstacles, including fear, negativity, threats, or betrayals.

OF SUDDEN REALIZATION, INSPIRATION, AND INSIGHT FROM 26 PROFESSIONAL MEN

Know Your Strengths and Weaknesses

Once you've set your objectives, you need to acknowledge your own strengths and weaknesses, or deficiencies, and defer or delegate tasks that you may not be suited to or capable of, or tasks that you do not enjoy doing. I believe one should spend 80% of their time doing things that they are proficient in and enjoy, for the simple reason that when you enjoy what you are doing, you become that much better at it, and thus your operation should become more efficient and productive. It is also important to know your own qualities so you can take into advantage of your own strengths and avoid stumbling over your deficiencies as you take action. This isn't a green light to settle and preserve your deficiencies—there is always room for improvement. You should simply allocate your focus, time, and energy in the right places, efficiently.

Ask and You Shall Receive

Call it the law of attraction, confidence, or whatever you like. Chances are, at some point in your life, you will want something but it won't just be given to you on a silver platter. You might have to hustle a little to get things done. In my case, whether you need website content from a client, a payment that is due, or a signed contract, you have to learn how to ask. In addition, you need to be able to ask for help and trust others. In my case, as a business owner, it took me a while to be able to entrust others with work that needed to get done, payments that needed to be made, etc. After all, I was a one-man show when I started my business!

Do Your Best and You Will Have No Regrets

My grandmother once told me something simple but

extremely important to me. She told me to do my best no matter what, in every given circumstance, and I will have no regrets. I have applied this to pretty much every area of my life, and it has been working out amazingly well. You must also not be afraid to dream big due to fear of failure. For instance, if you are currently earning $50,000 and set an objective to earn $100,000 next year, but you only make $90,000, that's still pretty good, right? Better yet, if your objective is to hit $1,000,000 and you only get halfway there, you're still making $500,000.

Being positive and setting proper objectives is key. Looking at this principle from another angle, you might decide that you want to get married and tell yourself that you would like to find a suitable life partner within one year. If it winds up taking two years instead, that's still pretty damn good! Dream big and take big actions!

Bio of Andreas Deligeorge

Andreas Deligeorge was born and raised in Montreal and is proud to be one of the first-generation Canadians among his family members of Greek and Hungarian origin. His hobbies include working out, playing soccer, and rollerblading. Fortunately for him, his online business, Omnivision Design (OmnivisionDesign.com) allows him the flexibility to continue to enjoy warmer climates throughout the course of the lengthy Canadian winters.

Andreas began his studies in the illustration and design program at Dawson College, and he complemented these studies with a certification in communications and marketing at Concordia University. He went on to work in e-learning, online payment processing, affiliate marketing, and search engine optimization while actively seeking contracts and acquiring additional experience running his growing web design and online marketing business. Eventually, he set up shop and launched the business full time, enjoying a flexible, innovative, work-from-home career.

Omnivision Design takes on contracts internationally and employs an increasing number of people in content writing, search engine optimization, web design, web development, video production, and print.

Foundation, Motivation, Education, and Favor
Rick Sinkfield, AIA

Growing up in the Washington, DC, Sinkfield house was a unique experience, I later came to realize. I was always told that all Sinkfields in the DC phone book were in my family. It had to be true since there were only four and I knew them all – my mom, my dad, my aunt, and a cousin. I was born at Freedman's Hospital while my parents lived in an apartment near Howard University. They soon moved to a row house in a Northwest DC community called Columbia Heights on a dead-end street bounded by Rock Creek Park, so I had plenty of room to grow and explore. Five years later, my brother was born. The house worked well for us and was in a great location—we could walk twenty yards to the corner, catch a bus to anywhere, walk to school, or even enjoy the park down the street. The zoo, memorials, museums, and cultural sites were all accessible to us—it was pretty cool!

My dad, a hard-working civil servant, was the dominant character in the house and Mom laid out the love. His socially-expected, self-appointed roles around the house included fixing any broken thing requiring tools or hardware, being the disciplinarian, and watching TV (including boxing, variety shows, the news, and any show with black people in it). He also knew and enjoyed anything Hollywood—actors, actresses, producers, or films (black or white, silent or talkie, he knew them all). He was known to take us to the movie theater on a weeknight; never mind the movie's scheduled start time, we'd arrive in the middle, stay until it started again, and then sleep to the middle. Somehow he'd wake up and say: "It's time to go home, boys. Let's go."

He was very outgoing and knew everyone in the neighborhood. He even enjoyed going to the grocery store, where he could interact with a broader network of like-minded friends. Anyone walking by the house got a greeting and even a prolonged conversation about any subject from weather to current events. He was a solid provider, working at the Bureau of Engraving for most of my school years. As a product of the Depression, he held many jobs from janitor to truck driver and he was always prepared to move forward in his career. Armed with a "head for numbers," a high-school education, and a passing score on the civil service exam, he finally landed that prized job with the federal government. Working for the government was highly desired by many blacks in the post-Depression era; it was stable, fair, and offered a good retirement. Over the years, he advanced from a cleaning man to a supply clerk.

Mom, an elementary school teacher with multiple degrees in education, had the fair complexion that probably gave her an edge in society back then. Her parents believed in taking advantage of all your talents and supported her through DC Teachers College. Early on, she sought to work for the government and landed a clerical job, but after a short time, she moved to teaching to match her academic preparation. She was a very caring and devoted teacher, and studied children's learning styles and techniques to accommodate them. She was from a family of educators, and she was very close to her only sister, a classroom teacher, and her husband, a middle school administrator. Her domestic skills were top-notch and broad. She could sew, cook, clean, manage the house, and even keep children in line with a firm whisper or just a smile.

My parents came to know each other through the church. It was there that they met and continued that connection, and even had the pastor officiate the wedding. My mother's dad was a frustrated, stern disciplinarian who had to tone it back since he had just the two daughters—he wanted to yell, but his wife wasn't having it for the two girls.

I was getting used to having full reign of the house until my brother showed up. All of a sudden, accommodations had to be made and I had to reluctantly give up some quality time with Mom. At the start, I wasn't pleased and acted out to get attention but as the years went by, I began to appreciate this new life in the house. He deflected some of the parental ire, gave me some time alone when I needed some, and caused some doubt as to who caused trouble—him or me. Later on, I came to respect him because he was very good with finances, had a high-tech mind, and was a good student.

Down deep, Dad really cared for us but had trouble showing it. I believe he was internally conflicted, having observed his own dad giving his sister the royal treatment while the boys got the business. That could have been the prevailing child-rearing technique back in the day, and he could care less about those newfangled Dr. Spock techniques, so he continued the tradition on us. He was very argumentative, so much so that he didn't even need someone to oppose him; he would still loudly argue the point on his own. He was mostly talk, except when he wanted to make a point with me and/or my brother. If we somehow got out of line, we'd have to find a "switch" [a springy twig from the yard], bring it back, and take our medicine. He once explained to us that his father was very strict on him and his two brothers, but not his sister. Fear of spanking and shouting were the constants.

Mom sought to tolerate the arguing while performing the expected role involving nurture, motherhood, and tenderness in the house. It was hard to take for her. She was just such a gentle soul that she felt she could melt you with her kindness. She was special.

After living in other places around the nation and visiting other countries in adulthood, I realized what it meant to grow up in Washington, DC, during that era. Our neighborhood, and the city overall, was not very racially diverse. The population was maybe seventy percent black, with pockets of whites or token whites scattered about. It was "chocolate city"! You could pause at the stoplight and see blacks in the car on the left and blacks in the car on the right. The city was diverse among blacks in that you could find pockets of poor, countrified, sophisticated, educated, well-to-do, well-heeled, and the wannabes. There were not many blacks with political or economic power, but that was turning itself around. Blacks were knowledgeable and demanding. They reasoned that the American Dream should happen for all, not just a few. It was a transitional time of renaissance, civil rights, and self-realization.

Still a young person, I didn't detect all this at the time. I didn't have the historical perspective or the situational awareness to realize the significance of all that was going on. There were clues, however. If you could synthesize all of it, all you had to do was listen to the news or read the Washington Post newspaper. We lived down the street from the seat of national power, a few blocks from the great thinkers of our world, around the corner from some of the great leaders of our time, and next door to the next generation of folks preparing to bring us forward as a civilization.

The Civil Rights narrative was violent action or nonviolent protests; political action or demonstrations; peace marches or Black Panthers. There were horrifying events in our nation occurring at that time—for example, the assassinations of President John F. Kennedy, Senator Robert Kennedy, and Malcolm X. War and the threat of war were in our consciousness. When the assassination of Dr. Martin Luther King Jr. occurred, the civil rights powder keg exploded into riots and looting in the streets. On television, I could see the same fires and looting I could see from my bedroom window up by the bus stop. This was scary and did not match any logic I could lay out; rather, I thought, this was an outburst of instinctive fear, frustration, and injustice that needed rectification. Again, I thought, this was a self-destructive reaction and there must be a better way.

High school was a point of awareness for me that took me to my next level of self-awareness. While youngsters of this age are reaching a stage of maturation, high hormonal levels, and brain development, faculty and parents are seeking ways to expose them to every experience available. I had a great set of supporters, and Washington, DC, was a great laboratory for broadening experiences.

I struggled through many of my math classes mainly for not applying myself. I enjoyed the things that came easy but shunned the things that required multiple levels of hard work. Mom helped me see the value of working through the problems and even demonstrated the gratification of a difficult problem solved by working through each step to completion. I also had a cousin, four years my senior, who was there to help. Aside from my parents, my cousin proved to be my most significant role model: he was a college student, an architecture major, and very astute in math. Algebra, algebra 2, and trigonometry were not easy, but I managed to get through them, achieving higher-than-average grades.

All math courses were a push until I came upon solid geometry: mathematics concerned with questions of shape, size, relative position of figures, and the properties of space. Somehow I was able to visualize each problem, each solution, and each answer before ever placing pencil to paper. Here was a math course that connected with real-world images in my mind. The teacher could send me to the chalkboard, hit me cold with a new problem, and I could hammer it out right there at the board.

Our high school was set up with courses for vocational careers, college-bound students, and business careers. Regardless of which track we were on, we were encouraged to take courses from each track to round out and broaden our interests. With a recommendation from my architecture-student cousin, I signed up to take mechanical drawing. It was mostly easy to me and, while I thought I was the best in the class, I discovered this cute, petite girl was out-drawing me with greater speed and accuracy than I ever thought possible. This brought out my competitive nature—I was not going to let this little girl beat me out in this course. I pushed myself in silence trying to beat her out without even letting her know I was in competition with her until one day I told her she was going down. To my surprise, she didn't really care about competing. She was just determined to do what came naturally and do her best. I connected with her many years later. I told her she was a catalyst in my going into architecture. We both had to laugh out loud.

Our high school also had a Junior Reserve Officer Training Corps (JROTC) detachment. With a few exceptions, JROTC was a requirement for all boys at the time. This was a great outlet for us; we got some real-life training that had a real purpose. We learned discipline, teamwork, marksmanship, weaponry, orienteering (map reading), military history, drill, and ceremonies. We had top-notch instruction from battle-hardened military men who did not tolerate bad behavior. If there was a hint of a behavior problem, the guilty party plus the rest of his unit would have to "pay" for the infraction by marching for extra hours or assuming cleanup duty; there was a certain accountability in that model. I worked my way up through the ranks and became a cadet major battalion commander (that's me in front). I gained a great appreciation for our military, what they do, and how they preserve freedom for our country.

Equipped with some math knowledge, drawing skills, some

social skills, and some military exposure, I readied myself for college. My architecture-student cousin was about to graduate from Howard University and he was recommending that I study architecture. He showed me some of his projects, described his courses, talked about college life, and pointed out what was most important: studying what you are good at and what you enjoy. I researched many architecture schools around the country, but my dad reasoned, "Why go way away from home when there's a perfectly good architecture school twenty blocks from home?" With that line of reasoning, Howard made lots of sense. Going to Howard was a key decision that mapped my future, whichever direction I would choose.

The faculty at Howard were very concerned that all students learn both a skill for a lifetime (such as drafting) as well as theoretical aspects (such as architectural design) of the subject. They were very nurturing; that is, they were willing to take whatever time necessary to help us individually through the academic challenges that all students face. Howard was also a mecca for black cultural studies and was a focal point for many Civil Rights thought leaders. The students even mounted a take-over of the administration building to protest inaction to injustices happening nationally and on campus (such as the shootings on the Kent State campus). This was the environment of the time, but it had a lasting effect on us all.

Even though the military was unpopular at the time (perhaps because of the unpopular Vietnam War), I joined the Air Force Reserve Officer Training Corps (AFROTC), hoping to stay with what I had learned and enjoyed in high school. Again, we received top-notch instruction from highly trained military men who conveyed the virtues of military values and skills through all the years we were with them. As a bonus, many of us received scholarships and stipends to continue with the Air Force after graduation. Graduating from Howard as an architect and a commissioned Air Force officer were two of the highest honors I have ever received.

My first Air Force active duty assignment was as a base architect with the Civil Engineer Squadron at Lackland Air Force Base in San Antonio, Texas. From what I learned in grade school through my time at Howard, I was technically and militarily prepared to start my career with the Air Force and was assigned a very supportive supervisor who gave me larger and more high-profile projects as time went on. I was given more responsibilities, promotions, and offers for other assignments at other locations.

In San Antonio, I met and married a young lady from Texas, and within three years we started a family. She gave me stability and support, which enabled me to do many things that would not have been otherwise possible. I am deeply grateful to her for her support and her devotion to me and our family.

I also started or joined existing black cultural organizations at every base I was assigned to. At the time, commanders would get good evaluations from their superiors if they had a robust black history program. During duty time, I received leadership support to participate in and conduct Black History Month celebrations. The idea was to promote cultural awareness among all airmen, to help bring them together in a cohesive fighting force, and to wipe out ignorance about black culture. This aligned with my own personal mission and allowed me to become creative in helping to celebrate black culture in the workplace. We organized social events, scholarships, speakers, and luncheons to promote our mission.

After serving my initial commitment of time and starting a family, I decided to leave active duty, start a civilian career with the Air Force, and join the Air Force Reserves in a part-time role. My civilian career started with designing Air Force sports, recreation, and leisure facilities worldwide. Later, I was able to manage funding, design, and construction for Air Force mission facilities worldwide, such as medical, aviation, and housing. I then became the Air Force's sole technical writer of design criteria and unique requirements for Air Force facilities worldwide. In 2007, I became the Air Force Subject Matter Expert for Architecture Programs, also known as the "Architect of the Air Force."

From family life in Washington, DC, to what I learned in grade school, through my time at Howard, I feel blessed to have been able to express myself, my knowledge, and my talents freely in my world. Now, as an Air Force military and civilian retiree, I am able to practice architecture and participate in church and community organizations, such as Tuskegee Airmen Inc., to stay connected with architecture and the community service activities I enjoy so much.

Bio of Ralph Sinkfield, AIA

Ralph "Rick" Sinkfield, AIA, is a registered architect in the state of Texas and a retired Reserve Air Force Lieutenant Colonel. He holds a Bachelor of Architecture degree from Howard University, Washington, DC, and a Master of Arts in Management from the University of the Incarnate Word, San Antonio, Texas. He served as Architecture Subject Matter Expert and an architecture technical consultant for the US Air Force from 2007 to 2014. In that capacity, he managed design criteria and architectural education programs, and represented the Air Force in industry and Tri-Service technical forums.

From 2005 to 2007, he served as a senior architect at the Air Force Center for Environmental Excellence (AFCEE) at Brooks City-Base, Texas. In this position, he provided recommendations, advice, leadership, vision, and expertise on technical design and construction criteria and standards for AFCEE's customers worldwide. Further, he promoted design and construction excellence across the Air Force by formulating, implementing, managing, planning, directing, and controlling Air Force programs needed to execute its architectural design and construction initiatives.

His Air Force experience includes work as a civil engineering faculty program manager, project manager, design team leader, MILCON/NAF programmer, architect, interior designer, commercial kitchen designer, technical writer, and urban planner. From 1979 to 1992 and again in 2004 and 2005, he joined the Air Force Services Agency to supervise five architects in the Project Management Branch to manage design and construction of over $600 million in Air Force sports, leisure, and recreation projects.

As an architect at the Air Force Center for Environmental Excellence during 1992 to 2004, his duties and responsibilities included formulating design policy, defining standards, developing design principles, managing architect-engineer contracts, leading design assistance teams, facilitating architectural workshops, and establishing design processes. He served as technical authority on major Air Force design projects, training facilitator, consultant on advanced architectural practices, Air Force representative at design symposia, and specialist on state-of-the-art design techniques and practices. He managed educational and policy event projects such as the annual Air Force Architects Workshop, the Air Staff Design and Construction Roundtable, and the $600 million Air Force Fitness Center Master Plan. He has written, edited, and consulted on Air Force and Tri-Service publications such as the *Project Manager's Guide for Design and Construction*, the *AF Library Design Guide*, the *AF Temporary Lodging Facilities Design Guide*, and many others.

Early on, he worked in commercial architectural forms, served as community planner with ACTION/VISTA, and was the Air Force Reserve Mobilization Augmentee to the Base Civil Engineer Commander at Randolph Air Force Base, Texas, providing professional technical support on architectural, personnel, project management, protocol, and customer process issues. He is active in his church and the American Institute of Architects (AIA); he

has served as president of the Brooks African-American Cultural Association for nine years and is current president of the San Antonio Chapter, Tuskegee Airmen, Inc. He is married to the former Caroline Denmon of Giddings, Texas. They have three boys.

Contact
Rink Sinkfield, AIA
8252 Garden North Drive
San Antonio, TX 78266
rixsink@gmail.com

Purpose, Responsibility, Mentorship and Contribution
Louis O. Biggers

My journey toward manhood was paved with many *A-ha Moments* orchestrated by a God who had a plan for my life even before I was conceived. However, it's important to acknowledge and point out my role in the development process such that readers can understand the enormous power that resides within each of us to shape our destiny!

Looking back on my childhood, I was tremendously blessed to be raised in an environment filled with love and encouragement. I am the oldest son of five children, with an older sister, two younger sisters, and a baby brother. Being named after my father and being the oldest son conditioned me to look to my father as a role model.

A major *A-ha Moment* was the realization that my father played a major role early in my life that put me on the path to a greater self-awareness and understanding of manhood. My mom played an equally important role, providing context to what it meant to be a man and servant leader. My dad emphasized the importance and value of hard work, responsibility, and guarding my mind, and he instilled within me that I could be and do anything that I put my mind to. However, my mom, through her dedication to church and service, led me to understand the purpose for the hard work and the means to guide my thoughts and ultimately discover my purpose.

The earliest *A-ha Moment* occurred when I accepted Christ

as my Savior at the age of 14 and realized that God had a purpose for my life—to serve others and help them to achieve authentic success in their life. I acknowledged and accepted my role as a man called to serve and to lead others, not merely to serve myself. As a father of three boys, I am keenly aware of my purpose in serving others, beginning with my own family. I serve as a role model to raise the next generation of men to serve their family, community, country, and world as husbands, friends, mentors, and leaders, desiring to leave a lasting legacy of growth and prosperity—giving more than taking. I am blessed and eternally grateful to my parents for encouraging and shepherding my heart to lead me to Christ. I believe this is the greatest mission of manhood—to serve others and lead them to a fulfilled life in Christ!

The next significant *A-ha Moment* came when I acknowledged that I am responsible for my place in life—good or bad! I am fortunate to have had great role models all of my life, but I recognize the role that I played in this good fortune as well. I developed a love for psychology at an early age because my father would often share what he had studied on the subject, particularly as it related to controlling my mind and thoughts. I recall an exercise that had a lasting impact on my journey into manhood. My father pointed out that when asked to "identify all the blue objects in a room," your brain tunes in and is able to pick out those objects with relative ease, whereas previously they were ignored. This early lesson trained me to guard my mind and to take responsibility for who and what I allow to influence my thoughts.

So, armed with my purpose, I became focused on controlling the information that would guide my thoughts. As a result, I began to attract people into my life that would propel me toward the purpose I was pursuing—from guidance counselors to teachers to coaches to pastors to friends and other advisors along the way. I accepted responsibility for my successes and failures, realizing that my thought process had gotten me where I was presently in life. I recall a dialog with my dad who was complaining after getting a speeding ticket, arguing that "he wasn't the only one speeding." But he was in fact speeding. I resolved never to play the blame game, but to take responsibility for my actions, committing to make wise choices. As a role model for my boys and others, I don't want to be a reason for them to stumble by making excuses.

Men must accept that they are created with a purpose in mind and assume personal responsibility for their own success or failure. They must be responsible to control and to create, if necessary, the environment conducive to their growth and success. Choose wisely who to associate with and to follow, what books to read, what music to listen to, and what shows to watch. You are responsible for your choices, not your dad, your mom, your brother, your sister, or your wife. You choose!

I recall a mentor pointing out that a study of the word *information* can be broken down into IN, FORM, and ATION. What you take IN will FORM the beliefs that will govern the AcTIONs that you take. More than what others say about you, as a man, you need to guard what you say about you. There's nothing wrong with you. You were created with a purpose and you have all you need to do your part! Don't let others define you or limit your potential.

The next major *A-ha Moment* came during my senior year of college as I approached graduation. I graduated as valedictorian of my high school and earned a full ride to Virginia Tech, majoring in computer engineering, with the goal of starting my own business to use computers and technology to improve the lives of people. Having focused on the work to get my degree, I hadn't taken any courses to really prepare me to start a business. Fortunately, I was introduced to the Amway business through a colleague while interning at IBM. Through this home-based business, I learned the importance of mentorship, acquiring business acumen that gave me an advantage when I began my career in the high tech industry and more importantly providing access to mentors that helped me to acquire skills necessary to develop and lead others—particularly men.

Over the years, I have been blessed to have received

mentorship advice from very successful individuals, including billionaires, each providing a slightly different perspective from which to draw as I approach life's many challenges. I have been able to draw upon their advice and wisdom to achieve success in my professional career and my personal life. Mentors help you to uncover the blind spots that you otherwise would not see, but that often limit your success.

One of the greatest hindrances to a successful transition to manhood is that most men lack accountability and mentorship with other men of honor. While others have shied away from network marketing for various reasons, I recognized it as the perfect vehicle for me to establish mentorship with others who had a vested interest in my success, which I recognized would only come through personal development and growth. The need for mentorship is so great that I formed Camelot Network to leverage the power of network marketing to develop servant leaders and to equip them to serve others in developing a lasting legacy to impact the lives of millions of people around the world.

My journey in network marketing has led to many more A-ha Moments—likely the result of being in an environment ripe with opportunities to learn from people from all walks of life. The most relevant *A-ha Moment* has been the realization that most people, men in particular, desire to be significant, recognized, and respected—whether for the accumulation of knowledge, money, automobiles, or even women—yet few obtain fulfillment and struggle throughout much of life. Fulfillment comes through growth and contribution and typically requires resources from and involvement with others beyond oneself. This is why it is important for men to be a part of a team or organization such that they can be a part of something bigger than just themselves.

As men, we are called to be servant leaders, serving mankind and growing personally to gain more in order to give more and thereby contribute to the betterment of society—present and future. Look to serve first, rather than be served. Serve God.

Serve your wife, your parents, and your kids. Serve your church, your neighbors, and your community. The greater your sphere of contribution, the more you are likely to act. Each opportunity to serve others that I accepted has led to greater opportunities to serve even more people—from volunteering to leading small groups at church in biblical stewardship or parenting to writing business plans to helping nonprofits launch sustainable social enterprises. Regardless of where you choose to serve, the world needs more men willing to serve to leave a positive and lasting legacy for future generations.

So, I implore every man to find his purpose and take personal responsibility for making the necessary choices to make it a reality. Focus on fulfilling your destiny and welcome potential mentors into your life, and submit to them when they offer you advice to further you along your journey to manhood. Reach out to other men to find an accountability partner to strengthen one another. But stay in your lane and avoid comparing your progress to that of others; we each have our own journey of discovery. Become a servant leader with a passion to serve and help others, rather than to be served. In doing so, you will be fulfilled as a man, making a significant contribution to society and leaving a lasting legacy for others to follow because of your example. Have fun and enjoy the journey!

Bio of Louis O. Biggers, MBA

Louis has over 20 years of experience in the technology industry, where he has held positions in engineering, planning, marketing, and strategy. He is also a credentialed Project Management Professional.

Louis graduated from Virginia Tech in 1994 with a bachelor's degree in computer engineering and a minor in computer science. He earned a master's degree in business administration from University of California, Davis, in 2008, with an emphasis on marketing, strategy, finance, and entrepreneurship.

Besides his love for technology, Louis has a passion for service and servant leadership, motivated first through service to his lovely wife and three boys.

He and his wife, Amy, have led small groups on parenting as well as biblical stewardship, and he still volunteers his time in the church nursery.

Louis is a member of the board of directors for Joy's G.I.F.T. and serves as the finance chair of the Women & Youth Empowerment Organization, whose mission is to inspire others in overcoming adversity through mental, emotional, and spiritual healing.

Louis is also co-founder of UNLEASH, through which he leads a team of MBA graduates who do business consulting in the Sacramento area. He and his team have provided consulting services and written business plans to enable nonprofits to launch several successful social enterprises.

He is a graduate of the Leadership Sacramento class of 2014, which raised over $125,000 in cash donations and received the same in in-kind donations to rebrand the Boys and Girls Club of Sacramento, changing it into a teen center.

Louis is also the founder of Camelot Network, a network of servant leaders committed and accountable to mentoring, coaching, and otherwise leading others to achieve authentic success in all areas of their life. Through Camelot Network, he is able to develop servant leaders and to enable them to serve others in developing a lasting legacy, impacting the lives of people around the world.

The Choices We Make
James T. Worthy

My name is James T. Worthy. I am 65 years old, born February 12, 1949.

The topic of my *A-ha Moment* is choices in life. I am the third oldest of 10 siblings, I have 4 sisters and 5 brothers, and my parents were my main teachers in life. In my early years, my parents were in constant teaching mode with all the children—there was a lot of teaching going on. My father was pretty much a disciplinarian. He did not have a whole lot to say—the words were spared at the end—but he had made his points and that was it. My mother did the main teaching. One thing that I do know is that I recalled and remembered what was taught. Not that I always followed it, but I do remember what I was taught. This principle has followed me through life. In my early years, like most kids, I was hard-headed. I would try things and I would fail a lot of the time, but that did not keep me from trying. I got along well with my siblings. We were a tight group. We were poor, but we didn't know we were poor. But we were happy—very happy. Even in times when it came to be punished, or during moments of crying and being upset over being teased, your pain was short-lived. Our good times together took all the energies from being sad and angry away from what you were angry at and it burst out into laughter because of what my other siblings would do around you. So we had a good time growing up.

I was very observant as a young person—very observant. I looked around at others, watching them. Sometimes I didn't know right away what I was watching, but I did a lot of that. I was very competitive with my brothers and sisters, with others, and with myself. I always pushed myself to climb higher and faster, to do more, and I did not see anything wrong with that. Growing into high school, my competitive juices flowed even more. I was able to not only be observant , but also be willing to participate. No matter what someone needed a participant for, I would see whether I could do it. I was still being taught lessons by my mother because my father spent a lot of time working. He chose to speak to us because he only had a third-grade education, he had a terrible time reading, and it was even harder for him to write. So we never pressed him to do any of that. I could see that in reading one sentence, he was working up a sweat. So reading wasn't something that we would see him do often, and that was something that would stay with me.

Life was going on, and I was called into the military. Many of life's experiences would come into play and help me to become the person I wanted to become. Without my knowing it, a lot of the teaching I got from my mother would come into play as I recalled these lessons. I was taught to always respect my elders and others.

My mother preached that we're all God's children. We're all human beings. I never heard her speak badly of another person. My mother is an amazing person. She was one of the greatest people I've ever known, a loving and caring person. I remember thinking as I grew that I hope I'm that patient and that kind with others—not because I wanted something in return, but because I could see how that made me feel about my mother being that kind of person and I thought that this would make me feel good about myself.

So I got into the military to begin my training. It would have a great impact on me, and it started with being pushed and shouted at and yelled at. On the first day, everyone was treated the same, not as individuals. It upset me, and it bothered me. I remember the day my platoon sergeant took everyone upstairs and said, "Who thinks he is the toughest in this room?" In my anger, I said, "I am the toughest in this room," while hearing some thirty guys say, "You are, drill sergeant, sir." I did not divert my eyes from anybody in the room because I did make a statement. And I looked at the drill sergeant and he walked toward me and I remember thinking, I'm in trouble now. He walked right up to me in my space and he said to me, "You're going to be my platoon leader." And my answer was, "Yes, sir, platoon leader." He did not ask me if I wanted to be, but he told me that I was going to be.

I remember lying in my bed that night, thinking about what I had accepted. And that was a large responsibility. I was going to be responsible for the functions of 39 other guys in my platoon, which also meant that I was going to be looked at as a leader and I had to lead by example. I was taught to lead by example. So, here is where I started in my first real leadership role. Prior to being selected, I did not stick my chest out and say, "I am the best leader." Once the drill sergeant chose me, I made the choice to be the best leader I could be, to lead by example. I didn't do things to say, "Look what I can do!" I would do the best that I could do and be satisfied with that.

If there's someone better, that's fine. If I did the best I could do and helped the other guys who needed help in any way, then fine, I was doing my job. It was one of the best experiences I could have had or been put in because at the time, being in the middle of the Vietnam conflict, perhaps that meant I would be in that same position one day in a country far from where I grew up. To me, it might not be a given, and I might not return from that country. I took the position that I was going to learn as much as I possibly could.

So during the course of our training, there were a number of incidents that happened to me that I had to think about before I responded. That was not an easy thing to do during that time in my life, but it was an important thing to do and it kept me from making mistakes that I would regret or become very embarrassed about. It all came back from the earlier teachings of my parents. I had not given much thought to when they would come into play in my life, but they did. The time would come when I would make more choices in my life, and I would learn that it made me the person I wanted to be.

Bio of James T. Worthy

Jim Worthy is a Vietnam veteran and a retired fireman who lives in Ohio. He has been involved in community work in Ohio and is one of 10 siblings.

A-ha Moments[1]
Ricardo McCrae

Gloria: What are your early childhood memories that shaped who you are as a man today?

Ricardo: My childhood was really marked by polar opposites. I will tell you what I mean by that. Until I was 10, I grew up in Guyana, South America, with tremendous wealth. My dad was a diplomat in the bauxite industry in Guyana. We lived in a gated community. There were Germans on one side and Indian people on other side of us. It was a gated community with blacks and whites. Everyone lived there who was in a certain class within the community, and I knew that we had a certain respect from everyone in that community. Even though we had a private pool, maids, a five-bedroom house, drivers, and five baths that my mom designed because she is an architect, we had all the trappings of wealth. From that I got an incredible sense of pride and belonging, an incredible sense of who I am and my worth in the world, the respect that I carry myself with, and dignity.

What I also experienced during that time was incredible abuse. My dad was violent toward all of the children, my brother and sister, as well as very violent toward my mom. I had this juxtaposition of having what I thought was normal, that everybody lived like that, and I did not know any better. But I

---

1 As interviewed by his wife and business partner, Gloria Roheim Mc-Crae

also had this tension whenever he was in the house and this sort of fear that you were always living with, that, "Oh my God, what is going to happen?" I remember very early on getting a compass and drawing a truck on his brand new "fridge" with a compass, etching it right into the enamel, and I got the beating of my life because of that.

Gloria: How old were you?

Ricardo: I was about four or five years old, and that really shaped me because I was just trying to draw. I learned that I could draw, and to then to get that kind of beating because I was trying to show you something that I drew, it just did not make sense to me. It really shaped me, and it left a clear message to me that art and creativity is not a good thing.

Contrast that with years later when my mom left my dad. She grabbed her three kids, flew out of the country, and went to live back home in Trinidad. So now, I am living with a single mom and two other kids. She worked as a teacher and eventually she got a job, trying to raise three kids on a teacher's salary in Trinidad and no experience with this flip side of the coin of poverty and actually not having anything.

Gloria: How did that shape your sense of being a man as a young boy?

Ricardo: Well, I still had that sense of how great I was. Not to be boastful, but I knew I was worthy, like I always knew that there was something in me that was great, and I was proud and I held my head high. Whether I had lunch to carry to school or not, I knew I was great. I just knew it. I was just like, I have got more in me. I did not allow those circumstances to dictate who I was. I knew I was different than my circumstances.

Gloria: Where do you think that came from?

Ricardo: From the experiences of seeing my grandfather. I was apprenticing in his watch repair store when I was younger, when he would come for visits. He was a man who was very well respected in Trinidad and to this day, his name still holds a lot of weight, even though he passed many years ago. The respect and reverence that people had for him wasn't because he was the wealthiest man, although he lived a very good life. He was a third-generation businessperson, but he respected people and people respected him. He would always walk in and say "good morning" or "good afternoon," and he would look everyone in the eyes and shake their hands. It did not matter if you were a banker or a beggar, he gave you the same respect. He gave everyone respect. He was loved by people. He would always say, "Treat people with respect. They deserve it." I would see him there, and sometimes people would come in the store to get something fixed, and some people could not pay and he would give them terms to pay later on. Or somebody would come in and they would say, "Why do I have to pay you so much to fix my watch?" He would say, "Well, you can pay me or you can go fix it yourself, and I am the only person who can do this right now, so that's the price." And they would say "okay" and they would pay. I saw him not use force to be a man, but use his intelligence, his charm, and his creativity, and that's where I really started to emulate him. I can identify with somebody who resonates with what I thought a real man was like and what the power of that was like, because I was also sensitive and caring and artistic and that really resonated with me as a young man.

Gloria: So you have two somewhat and in many ways

opposing...

Ricardo: Yes, polar opposites really.

Gloria: Both still dignified and respected professional men, but different in their being and different in their essence. When did you recall as a kid the first time you really acknowledged that you were a man?

Ricardo: (Long pause and several deep breaths). I knew there were two times, specifically, that I knew I was a man. It comes from a boom and an echo. What I put out and what the world gives back to me. There were two very clear moments in my life when I knew something had changed and I was no longer the same. I always felt like I was "grown," but when I turned 19, I was in a high school in Oshawa, Ontario, a small town outside the city of Toronto. I had my first girlfriend. At first, we were friends and everything was fine with her parents. She was Polish. When we became boyfriend and girlfriend, everything changed. Her dad changed, her mother, her grandma, everybody. I had just turned 18 or 19 years old, and I had just started sort of maturing as a man, because I tend to look very young and youthful and charming.

Gloria: (giggles)

Ricardo: The minute I became a boyfriend, everything changed. People looked at me differently, everything changed.

Gloria: What were some of those obvious changes? What did it go from and to?

Ricardo: It went from yeah, it's no problem, it's nice Ricardo, to what the f—k are you doing in my house. Like, you are with my daughter and that's a whole different ballgame. That was a striking moment for me that changed. The second thing that really changed, when I knew there was like a definite switch, was when I first shaved my head back in '92 before it was even popular. I was in arts school and I figured, hey, I will just shave my head. Shaving your head was not cool back in '92, and the world treated me differently. Like when I went out, and hung out with my friends and we would go to a club or be hanging out or whatever. Women treated me differently, men treated me differently, everyone. It was like living in someone else's body. It was a sense of like "okay, watch out now."

Gloria: So what did that say to you about you being a man? Or what did you interpret from that about your manhood, if anything?

Ricardo: I interpreted that I was being treated as a man, even though I did not feel like one.

Gloria: And what is a man?

Ricardo: A man? The word that comes to me is gracious. A man is confident and gracious, and with grace, I mean you don't have to put someone down so that you can stand up. You can stand on your own and you can be proud and be gracious with people. Now, that is a man and that is a powerful man. A man that has to stand up and put someone down is actually afraid. He is afraid of being found out that he is not really a man.

When you are truly a man, you are confident and gracious with people.

Gloria: And I think you can see that all over your life today, but I am curious about why that's your definition of a man. When you say you realized that you were a man because of how people treated you, it did not sound like they assumed you were being gracious and caring. What attributes of men did you feel that they imposed on you from the outside when you shaved your head, when you became a boyfriend?

Ricardo: Threatening.

Gloria: So, a man is threatening?

Ricardo: I felt that they felt that I was threatening. I became threatening when I shaved my head. I became threatening when I dated their daughter. I was no longer asexual. It was clear that they had an idea what a man was, and I fit that description.

Gloria: And when you say that perception included a man being threatening, what did you feel that was like when you had that put on you?

Ricardo: I describe it like having an evil twin brother who is going around causing all sorts of trouble and doing all sorts of things. As soon as the trouble happens, he runs and you are standing there and they say, "Hey, woah, that's him," and you say, "What's going on?" and you start explaining that you have a twin, that it's not really you, and blah, blah, blah, blah, blah. It's dealing with the legacy and thoughts of who black men are in the world, and I just actually have to deal with their interpretation of that. I just can't be a sensitive, gracious, and caring man. I literally have to deal with their ideas of whatever they have in their head and dance with that.

Gloria: So to pull it all together, thinking about your childhood and all those early experiences that shaped you as the man you are today, how do you see all of those experiences? You realized those moments when you were a man in your adolescence, seeing your grandfather and your father—everything from brutality to compassion and kindness—where do you see remnants of this shaping you in the way you are a man today?

Ricardo: It drew two lines in the sand. They were both realities. They were both very present in my life. You can choose, and that's how life actually showed up for me. You can choose to be like this and have success and have money and brutalize people and be the alpha male, or you can choose to be like this and be respected and have money and be a sensitive, gracious, caring man who is actually deeply respected by people. Now, there is respect and there is fear. People feared my dad; people respected my grandfather. Even after his passing, people respect his name and what he stood for. Now that is far more long lasting, far more powerful, palpable, and real because if you have no longer have to do anything to get respect from people, that is truly manhood. That is truly living a powerful, great life to the point where he didn't believe in insurance and his store burned down and someone…

Gloria: Who is he?

Ricardo: My grandfather. Someone gave him a location to open a store. Because of the man he was. Someone said "Na na na na, that can't happen to you. Here, why don't you have a piece of something and open the store here?" and he just gave it to him because of his character and the goodwill that he created in the world by being loving and gracious. It's something that I still hold very near and dear to my heart today—the act of being a loving, gracious man.

Gloria: Your sense of manhood is not tainted by the portrayal of men—particularly, black men, power, aggression, force, brutality—those types of things that are often portrayed. You even did see one side of your own father growing up, but you chose something else. You saw it growing up. You knew it was possible.

Ricardo: Yeah, I know it is possible. I always believed this: if you can conceive or think of something, you can actually do it. I think it is physically impossible to think of something and not be able to do it. If you can think of grace, you can think of love, you can do it. If you can think of violence, hatred, and aggression, you can do that as well. As humans, we have this choice to make.

Gloria: What was it like for you to choose a less conventional narrative of a man?

Ricardo: It was hard at times, many, many times. It is challenging to people when they are "different," but it is also challenging for me to live in that box they want me to live in, because that also comes with a series of burdens and constraints, but they are constraints on my life and what I am here to do.

I know that if I believe in being gracious and I am going to be gracious, if it upsets a lot of people, it's okay. I am happy with me, and I do not need you to like me. I am not going to make myself unhappy so you can have a moment of peace in your world or some fantasy you have about me that is not even real. So, I decide how I live and how I act and then the world will do what it does.

I am going to be me.

Gloria: That's a great way to end.

Ricardo: Thank you.

Bio of Ricardo McCrae

Ricardo is the Chief Artistic Officer and co-founder of Wedge15 Inc. and the Executive Director of WhosWhoinBlackCanada.com. With a background in fine arts and over a decade of corporate sales and project management experience, Ricardo is an original business artist, a passionate and creative professional. He has a unique way of combining the best of art and business to produce remarkable results for his clients.

Before partnering with his wife, Gloria, in Wedge15, his Ricardo McRae Agency led over 175 successful projects for its clients across virtually all sectors: nonprofit, entertainment, financial services, legal services, B2B, clean technology, consumer services, creative services, health and beauty, and media and publishing.

His designs have been featured in *Canadian Business Magazine*, the Photoshop conference in Boston, and twice by software developers as cutting edge web design. Ricardo has been using social media to connect and engage people for over a decade.

His blog, HookMeUpRico.com, has 6,000 longtime members that network and share with one another. He was also responsible for the 5,000-person flash mob Moonwalk for Michael Jackson (https://youtu.be/rF6B3_yfUF0) in 2009, at Yonge and Dundas Square.

Despite years of service to his community, Ricardo was still frustrated by the inaccurate portrayal of black Canadians, so he co-founded WhosWhoinBlackCanada.com, and today it's the only national platform profiling black excellence in Canada. The website, with 290 profiles to date, gets 30,000 visitors per month and is seen in over 100 countries around the world.

Prior to beginning his dynamic career, Ricardo studied fine arts and business at the University of Windsor and at the Ontario College of Art and Design. He also earned both his project management and professional sales designations during his years as an account executive on Bay Street. Written up in The Huffington Post, he was referred to as a "New Radical," someone who does good at work.

A-ha Moments
Pharaoh Freeman

"PUT YOUR HANDS WHERE I CAN SEE THEM! AND GET OUT OF THE CAR!" Although it wasn't my first altercation with the law, something told me that this time it was going to be different...

The streets were lit up like a Christmas tree as police cars drove in from all directions, blocking me, my friends, and the person who owed me about $10,000. Unfortunately for us, we had placed the money in the back seat as we were heading for a "little drive." We were all placed face down on the grass as the police took the testimony from the so-called "victim." The next thing I knew, we were all in individual cells waiting for the "paddy wagon" to bring us to court.

Two years later, well over $10,000 in court fees, and charges of assault and kidnapping, I found myself with 240 community service hours, a new contact for tattoos, and under house arrest with a lot of time to reflect—18 months to be exact.

Twenty-four months after that, I was watching M'city SOLO (my younger brother, business partner, and co-convict) on stage in the gym at our high school, MacDonald High in St-Anne de Bellevue, as he performed. He ended his performance with a speech addressing the genocide that was currently going on in Darfur. As I watched him speak and I watched how captivated and attentive the students were, I had another *A-ha Moment* when the Music with Meaning tour was born. Because both of us couldn't travel to the US with our new criminal records, we had to be creative if we wanted our record label to succeed. With experience and charisma, we had opportunity.

M'city SOLO and I grew up in Pincourt, a very remote location west of the island of Montreal, Quebec, Canada. We went to a predominantly white elementary school. We would never have been introduced to certain genres of music had we not experienced what we called "the white influence."

My younger brother and I would spend Saturday mornings mastering the use of the chain saw as we cut firewood for the fireplace. When we lived in Pincourt, there was no transportation, so I would walk an hour from my house to the closest bus station just to be able to go see my friends on the island of Montreal—perseverance and discipline.

Okay, maybe spitting in the face of the bus driver for not letting me out at my stop was a little excessive, but at the time I had a very short fuse and it was clear that the driver wouldn't stop the bus because he had a problem with little black boys. Yes, eating next to the window of the local Wendy's as I was heading to work wasn't the best idea. A few weeks later, I found myself with my father at juvenile court being sentenced to community work. The Omni Center was the community center where I was sentenced to complete my service hours. Six months later, I was hired as their evening caretaker.

The Right Place at the Right Time

Throughout our life experiences, we go through ups and downs, and that's natural. What is not natural is when we interpret these life experiences as "negative" and "positive." We are the ones who determine how we will interpret a situation and, more importantly, how we react to the situation. The most valuable lesson I have learned from life (the best teacher) is to learn from every life experience—not judge it, not react to it, but pause in the moment, observe it, and learn from it. By taking that approach, you will benefit from all your experiences whether they are negative or positive.

That does not that mean everything in life will be easy and perfect, and you shouldn't want it to be. The reason I say that is because the "downs," or setbacks in life we go through, are essential for getting our attention. These experiences help us to realize we are doing something that is taking us away from our objective of living a great life experience. When everything is "too perfect," we as individuals have a tendency to become habitual and life becomes mundane. As soon as something comes along and creates contrast or conflict, it gets our focus. Most of us react to the contrast by reflex. We tend to blame others, get sad, get mad, or host an amazing pity party for ourselves. Perhaps the reason why all that contrast came into our lives was to put us back on course. What we deem negative, life deems necessary.

I am a spiritual counselor who helps people to understand themselves from the inside out. I am married to the love of my life, and we own a cottage in the woods. I have two children and a godson I love like my own. I co-own a record label, Tru Kings Records. I co-founded one of the most successful school tours impacting the lives of over 50,000 youth, Music with Meaning. I mentor youth, I run a home-schooling network, and I am the largest Canadian distributor of the documentary *Hidden Colors*, which teaches African history before slavery. I am also the founder of the OFC Community (One Full Circle Organization) where we focus on community building, unification, and empowerment. When I look back at some of my life experiences, everything I have gone through—experiences that most would consider "negative"—was necessary for me to become who I am today. Seeing how much I love life, can I call them "negative" or should I coin them as "blessings"? The choice is mine, and I say thank life for every single blessing I have. It isn't easy at first to keep a cool head when going through negative experiences, but practice makes perfect.

The choice will always be yours. You have to decide whether

you want to take the experience and cry about it, learn from it, sink because of it, or grow with it. If you look around, most people are literally dying as a result of "dis-ease," so if your objective is to live, do what you can at all costs to remain positive, joyful, peaceful, and feeling at ease. When you mess up (because you will), or when life throws you some difficulty (because it will), never dwell there. Pick yourself up, learn, grow, and keep moving with a smile on your face. Appreciate the contrast, no matter how bad, as a necessity for your ultimate wellbeing. The sooner we acknowledge that, the sooner we learn from the experience and evolve.

We are here to evolve, live, and grow. Life is about the journey, not the destination. Enjoy your journey!

Bio of Pharaoh Freeman

Spiritual Counselor and Speaker

Pharaoh Freeman is a devoted husband, celebrating seven years of beautiful marriage in October 2015, father to a son of six years and a daughter of three years, and godfather to a godson of nine years. At the current age of 33 years, Pharaoh Freeman is now only beginning his life experience.

From the age of seven years, Pharaoh has always had a natural gift to speak and a genuine desire to help others. So it was no surprise when he decided to use his extensive network of people and businesses to launch The One Full Circle (OFC) networking agency and mentorship group, designed to help empower and unite the black community. With the slogan "Empowering & Uniting to Strengthen & Rise" and more than 150 members since its launch, the OFC organization is being true to its mission.

Aside from running the network, Pharaoh enjoys being a spiritual counselor, working within the community, and homeschooling his children, and he and his wife also provide the tools necessary for other parents within OFC to do the same. In addition to that, with the help of the first two parts of the documentary *Hidden Colors*, he's dedicated to speaking at public and private functions, where he combines the content from the documentary and his heightened sense of spirituality, his "overstanding" of life, and his knowledge of African history and culture to help people achieve success in their lives.

It is all about a positive and powerful self-image, but if you don't respect where you're coming from as an African king or queen, you'll never get to where you want to go. Solely making money is no longer his motivation. Pharaoh feels so much more fulfilled knowing that he has helped a brother or sister to understand themselves and made a positive difference on the planet.

Launching OFC is just the beginning for Pharaoh Freeman. OFC is dedicated to its people and will not stop until all black people overstand that unity is the key, educating their own children is success, supporting their own businesses is financial freedom, and strong families will create a strong nation.

Pharaoh is on call by referral only.

Contact TheOFC.org or Pharaoh.Freeman@gmail.com.

OF SUDDEN REALIZATION, INSPIRATION, AND INSIGHT FROM 26 PROFESSIONAL MEN

My A-ha Moment
Marc Garfinkle

I am white and Jewish, although some will say that cannot be. I grew up on the white side of a racially diverse small city and did not attend school with many students of other races until high school. My parents were not racist, but they had no black friends in their social circle.

Back then, in the 50s and 60s, when referring to people of African descent, polite whites said "colored people" or "Negro." So did polite Negroes. Hence, the National Association for the Advancement of Colored People and the United Negro College Fund had politically correct names at the time. Of course, the term of preference would later become people of color, black, Afro-American, Afro, African-American, or soul brothers/sisters, depending on where I was and when. It is often considered racist to use an outmoded term, even "colored people" and "Negro."

At home, Jews generally referred to blacks using the Yiddish word "*schvartze*," which means "black." That did not change so often. It was not a derogatory term. It was the correct word, perhaps the only word, they used in Yiddish. Of course, like most words, it can be derogatory, depending on the user—just like the word *Jew*. Although some prefer others to say, "He is Jewish," I never minded hearing, "He's a Jew," if the tone was not unkind. This is like today, with some political conservatives trying to make us think that "liberal" is an offensive word.

Despite the changing notion of propriety, the word "nigger" was never an appropriate term. I never heard it in our house and we never needed to be told not to say it. This fact gave rise to much reflection on my part about the connection between the word and the sentiment behind it. I was confused as to how to think about people who said it.

One of my mother's lifelong friends had married a guy named Eddie. He was fun to be with, and he was very always ready to help my un-handy father with home repairs; he was a true friend of the family. Apparently, one evening Eddie said the word and my mother immediately threw him out of the house. My parents would not let him back in until he agreed not to use that word in our home. I don't recall how long that took, although I remember being surprised at my parents' intolerance.

I was also surprised that my mother would jeopardize her relationship with her lifelong friend because of her husband's poorly chosen word. Did she oppose the word or the racism behind it? If Eddie was actually racist, then perhaps my parents were correct in no longer befriending him. But what if he were truly racist, but merely refrained from using the word out of respect for my parents? Did that make him more acceptable as a friend?

I later figured out that my parents found his racial intolerance to be ignorant and offensive, but if he kept it to himself, they could forgive his bias, much like my mother could forgive my father's offensive cigarette smoking, as long as he did it outside. I began thinking that perhaps we can still be friendly with people we know who harbor prejudices we don't share. I got to see this up close a few years later.

Part of my 19th summer was spent as a deck hand on a barge on the Ohio River. The captain and crew of eight or nine on my boat were mostly from West Virginia and Kentucky. I had never met the crew, and had only met the company owner before being hired.

I had not been on the boat for ten seconds when the captain

OF SUDDEN REALIZATION, INSPIRATION, AND INSIGHT FROM 26 PROFESSIONAL MEN

told me to lay my duffel bag down "alongside the niggerhead." I stopped in my tracks. In front of me, on the forward deck was a four-foot tall, bulbous black iron fixture which, I later learned, is also called a *capstan*. It is like a giant ratchet that tightens the cables that hold the barges together. I was a bit shocked at the term, but not unfamiliar with the ways of my Appalachian friends. I set my bag down alongside the thing.

I later learned that the captain was a good, God-fearing man who supported his family, never cheated on his wife, and didn't drink or smoke—though, like the rest of us, he "chawed t'bacca." He was honest and fair. He was generally not judgmental, and he was respected up and down the river. I suspected he shared some local prejudices.

Although I have always been proud of my Jewishness, I never mentioned it on the boat. Most of the crew had probably never met a Jew. Fortunately, I suppose, "Garfinkle" is not an identifiably Jewish name to people who don't know Jews. That probably saved me some grief, and it caused me to wonder whether it was okay to like these people, some of whom might have disliked me had they known I was Jewish.

One day, I was standing with the Captain on the gunwales of the towboat while we were out of the water on a repair dock near Pittsburgh. We were in "dry dock," but the crew had to remain on the boat. For hours, all around us, dozens of men, black and white, were scurrying around the shipyard doing their various jobs. Most of the men were wearing white hardhats. A few men were wearing yellow hats, obviously the supervisors or foremen.

Three of these yellow hardhats were standing talking together for a long time. Two of the men were white. One was black. They had been standing in one spot for hours as the workers hustled and bustled all around them. At one point, the captain walked by and stopped to watch the goings-on with me. Looking at the scene in front of us, he said to me, "Look at that nigger. He hasn't done anything all day!"

Although my immediate reaction was to point out that, "The white guys haven't done anything either," I paused to think before I spoke. I said nothing. I realized, "Here is a man who is so affected by stereotypes, and has so little contact with the people he stereotypes, that he doesn't really see the truth. He just *didn't even see* that the white guys were also doing nothing. He is just ignorant and blinded by his ignorance. I bet he really doesn't know any soul brothers at all." I wondered, "Should I dislike him for his prejudice or forgive him for his ignorance?" I chose the latter route.

Unfortunately, more and more Americans are allowing themselves to be defined by how they feel about one issue. For example, some people will not associate with people from another political party or people who don't share their feelings on issues like abortion, gun control, and the Middle East. This is a dangerous and fruitless attitude.

Each of us contains a little of the good, the bad, and the ugly. The better you know a person, the more of each aspect you will see. We say, "Accept people for what they are." That is difficult to do. Tolerate and accept the differences, even fundamental differences, between you and the people you are with. At home, in school, or at work, ignore or overlook what you don't like. Look for factors and forces that unite rather than divide you.

If you feel that you are subjected to bias, try to show by example the foolishness of that bias. Be better than they expect you to be. Be better than they *want* you to be. And don't reject them for their views. Reject only their views, if you must, but try to forgive their ignorance.

It may take some self-inspection, but you can learn to get along with, or even live on a crowded boat with, people whose prejudices you don't share. It is worth the effort to try.

Biography – Marc Garfinkle

(Marc@NJEthicsAttorney.com)

Marc Garfinkle is a longtime New Jersey civil and criminal trial attorney who now limits his practice to legal ethics, bar admission, judicial misconduct, and attorney discipline. In addition to his practice, Marc is currently serving as a municipal public defender in Livingston, New Jersey, and as an adjunct professor of persuasion and advocacy at Seton Hall University School of Law, where he instructs law students in pretrial advocacy on behalf of the National Institute for Trial Advocacy (NITA). Marc is a former New Jersey Attorney Ethics investigator and a past vice-chair and chair of the New Jersey Supreme Court District (VB) Attorney Ethics Committee.

Marc offers keynote talks, seminars, workshops, and retreats for lawyers and other professionals, focusing on persuasive speech. He has provided training to state bar associations from coast to coast and to government trial lawyers at the Department of Immigration and Customs Enforcement. His online professional education programs have been produced nationally by Lawline.com, West LegalEdcenter, Rocket CLE, and others.

He appears frequently in the media commenting on matters of legal ethics. He serves as a special legal ethics consultant for Thomson Reuters and writes regular legal ethics columns for the *New Jersey Law Journal* and the Essex County (NJ) Municipal Court Committee newsletter. He is a regular featured contributor to the California State Bar publication *Big News for Small Firms*.

A graduate of Marietta College in beautiful southeast Ohio, where he was briefly a scholastic debater (and was elected to Phi Beta Kappa), and Hastings College of the Law in San Francisco, where he enjoyed his education inside and outside of the classroom, Marc "hung out a shingle" in that city as soon as he was admitted to the California bar. Business was slow, at first. As a result, he had many interesting part-time jobs: in addition to the stint he spent "on the river" (discussed in his essay), he has been a private investigator, car detailer ("Simonize" Garfinkle), paid lecturer, English instructor, law instructor, door-to-door salesman, copy editor, finishing carpenter, and house painter.

Marc, who speaks French because of a fortunate marriage, believes that he became the first attorney in New Jersey to speak Haitian Creole back in the early 1980's. Since that time, he has become a fixture in that community. Over the years, Marc has been featured in numerous nonprofit television and radio shows in Creole, helping the underprivileged Haitian-American community with their daily lives and legal travails. He is grateful for the rare opportunity to be accepted so enthusiastically into this little-known and widely misunderstood subculture.

Marc was also counsel to the late, great heavyweight boxing

champion, "Smokin' Joe" Frazier, and he is thankful for his vistas into the sports and memorabilia subcultures as well.

A sole practitioner from the start, Marc shares some lessons and *caveats* from his experience in his popular, self-published book, *$olo Contendere: How to Go Directly from Law School into the Practice of Law without Getting a Job* (3d ed.) (Solo Contendere Press, 2010). The state bar associations of Ohio, Oregon, Missouri, and Colorado produce their own licensed versions, and Marc is invited frequently to speak to attorneys across the country about the topics in the book.

Marc has also written *The Law Enforcement Officer's Hip-Pocket Guide to Testifying in Court*, *The Hip-Pocket Guide to Testifying in Court*, *The New Lawyer's Hip-Pocket Guide to Appearing in Court*, and *The Hip-Pocket Guide to Speaking in Public*. ©2005, 2008, 2010, 2014 Hip-Pocket Guide Press, all rights reserved.

Marc lives with his wife of 30-something years, Eylana, in Livingston, New Jersey. He has two adult children, Yaël and Jordan, and a grandson, Avi. Marc likes to fish, garden, travel, and look at rocks. He would love to hear from friends, old and new.

My Name is Howie
Howard Blessing, DMD

My name is Howie, and I was named after my dad! I was always called "little Howie" and my dad was "big Howie." Most of my *A-ha Moments* revolve around being "little Howie."

I am not muscular, mechanically inclined, hairy-chested, well-endowed sexually, or interested in sports, and I am not a workaholic. For me, these *A-ha Moments* are more about the journey in being the "man" that I really am and the destination and connection I have about being a man.

I am the oldest boy of five children. We all grew up in the house that my dad was born in. I guess I would be called an "inner city" kid. His brother and family lived on the second floor and his parents lived on the first floor. I mostly played in the street with the other kids in the neighborhood. We were not rich and we were not poor.

My journey began when I started school and started being sexually abused by my older male cousin that lived on the second floor. When I would come home from school, he would wait for me and invite me in. I was about six at the time. It all began with him asking me about what kind of penis my dad had and if I would tell him about it. It progressed to having me perform fellatio on him. I saw my dad's penis while he was taking a bath. He was very well-endowed and uncut. I wondered why my penis didn't look at all like his. What was the matter with me? Am I not the "man" that I should be?

OF SUDDEN REALIZATION, INSPIRATION, AND INSIGHT FROM 26 PROFESSIONAL MEN

My abuse situation followed me for a very long time—almost 40 years. But that is another part of the story. I had no reference point about what is a normal penis for a man.

My first *A-ha Moment* happened when I was a pre-teen in the men's locker room at our community pool. I realized that my penis was pretty much "standard issue," even though I was "cut." In high school, my *A-ha Moment* was verified again. I still wish that I had been given the choice in being "cut."

I remember telling my parents about the abuse that was going on, and they told me never to tell anybody about it. That planted the seed that I had done something "bad." I was a "bad" person, and I longed to redeem myself.

My dad was a workaholic! He would come home from work and continue to work around the apartment house. He expected me to work with him in whatever capacity he chose. I was basically his slave. He had no friends. He didn't laugh, and he almost never talked to his brother or other people in his family. We mostly had fun with my mom's side of the family. She was one of ten kids, and everyone on her side of the family lived in town. I remember working with him in our back garage when I was about 16. I had no choice but to do whatever he said. All of a sudden, it hit me. I wanted to run away! I didn't want to be like him at all and I had no connection to my dad as a man. But where would I go? I was trapped!

My dad couldn't swim; he didn't like the sun or the heat. From that point on, I definitely wanted to do everything my dad didn't like to do just so I didn't have to be around him!

My mom's side of the family gave me my next *A-ha Moment*. She had lots of brothers who liked to have fun. For me, they were the real men. They got together every Sunday for a picnic, had a few beers, laughed a lot, and enjoyed not working. They became my role models for being a man. My uncles still get together and play golf even in their 80s. But I still had no "connection" to my dad—it was a "disconnect." So in high school, I offered to do all the outside work at the apartment. I was in my glory because I didn't have to interact with my dad. I wondered still what was wrong with me. My dad never taught me to play baseball, as he was never interested in sports. He wanted to work more than play. My grandfather (my dad's father) lived with my grandmother on the first floor (she died when I was about 16). My next *A-ha Moment* came from him.

    I never saw him angry. He always told great stories about his travels as a young man, and he was totally not like my father. So I hung around with him. I eventually lived with him when I went to dental school, as we both needed each other. He liked to fish, have a few drinks, and tell stories. He became my connection to being a "man." But why don't I have a connection to his son—my dad?

    I wanted still to please him, so I went to college and met a lot of people who helped to shape me into the person that I am today. It became more of a contest, to be better than he was. I was ready to "rub his face into it," as he never went to college. I still felt that there was something wrong with me. I must be still a "bad" person deep down inside of me. I wanted people to like me and it became my mission. I loved college and eventually went and graduated from dental school. After dental school, I became a commissioned officer with PHS, got married, and moved away. My father was devastated because he wanted me to open an office in town so he could brag about "my son, the dentist." I felt that I was finally good enough for him, but the disconnect continued.

    I had been married for about 25 years when I finally disclosed to my wife that I had been sexually abused as a child. I went to counseling and eventually told my parents about going to therapy. My dad was incensed. He said that the therapist must have planted that in my mind! I told him that I didn't want to talk to him or see him again. The disconnect got worse! It took a long time before my parents came to visit us. We already had children—two boys. Because of my past with my dad, I tried my best to have a connection with my wife and my boys. I never missed a swim meet

or a baseball game. During that visit, my dad and I were sitting outside by the pool. I like to be naked as much as I can. He took one look at me and said that "it was disgusting." Nice move, Dad! So we have another level of disconnect.

My next *A-ha Moment* came when my younger son got busted for weed. I was coming home just as the police were taking him away in handcuffs. My name was in the newspaper; he went on trial, got convicted, and was sentenced to a year in jail. I blamed myself for a long time because I was smoking weed when they were growing up and still do. As a man and father, I need to show my son that we are still connected, regardless of the situation. I never missed a visiting opportunity, as painful as it was.

My story will end soon. My mom died about 14 years ago of a massive heart attack. My dad was alone, and I was living in Washington State with my wife and family. When I was a kid, my family bought some land on a lake. You know the drill—I was slave labor again. My dad wanted to go to the lake at the end of the summer and my siblings couldn't take him. I offered to fly back and take him. By then, I was in my mid-fifties and had mellowed quite a bit. I bit the bullet and we both went to the lake. While we were there, I helped him with his garden. It needed to be tilled badly, so I got the rototiller out and took it up to the garden. We have the only camp on this pond, so I decided to till in the buff. My dad came up to the garden and instead of saying how disgusting that was, he laughed. He said that he had never seen anyone work nude in the garden. I finally realized a connection. We talked and he told stories like his father. He also talked about his younger sister, who was a "special needs" child who died before she was 20. He told stories about how he would stay home and take care of her so that his parents could go out and how this made him feel trapped. A-ha—another connection!

He died a few years later, and I was asked to give brief talk at his funeral. What could I say that would be meaningful? My message was simple. We sometimes go through life focusing on the "disconnect." For me, it was more important to focus on the "connection" with my father, as a man, no matter how hard it was or how long it took. For me, even though it took me almost my whole lifetime, the journey was well worth it because it helped shape me to be the man—the person—that I am today.

I have dedicated my life to helping people. I wouldn't have chosen my professional and personal path without the pain of being abused, without the disconnect with my father. I am proud of the man—the person—that I have become. These *A-ha Moments* are about my journey and the sense of peace that I feel. I hope you can all find it too!

Bio - Howard Blessing

Dr. Howard F. Blessing is currently a semi-retired dentist who lives for months in Walla Walla, Washington, and the remaining time in Lake Havasu City. While in Washington State, Dr. Blessing teaches the Public Health component in an Advanced Education in General Dentistry program sponsored by the University of Washington Dental School. He also contracts with the Washington Dental Service Foundation to teach medical residents, primary care medical providers, and other health professionals about the correlation between oral health and overall systemic health. In addition, he trains medical providers about the importance of risk and clinical assessment on young children during well-child checks and how to use fluoride varnish effectively in their practices. He is also a calibrated examiner for the Washington State Smile Survey.

Dr. Blessing was instrumental in developing multiple oral health coalitions in Washington State and has worked with many local health agencies in program planning, evaluation, and technical assistance. He is currently a life member of the ADA and the WSDA.

Dr. Blessing received a BS in biology from Marietta College in Marietta, Ohio, a DMD degree from the University of

Connecticut School of Dental Medicine, and an MPH from Loma Linda University. He became a commissioned officer in the United States Public Health Service upon graduating from dental school in 1974 and spent the next 26 years with the USPHS as a clinical dentist. He received both an Achievement and Commendation Medal from the USPHS and retired from the USPHS in 2000 with the rank of CAPT. His tours of duty included both Indian Health Service and National Health Service Corp assignments. During his assignment in Walla Walla, Washington, he was named outstanding dentist of the year by both the national MCH/ HeadStart and the regional HeadStart programs. After resigning his commission in 2000, he became the director of special dental programs for Yakima FarmWorker's Clinic and developed and implemented their current Mobile Unit Dental Program. He has since retired from YVFWC and contracts with them in the AEGD program.

Dr. Blessing has provided oral health services to close to a million people over his 40-year career. Many of those people were children and families with no access to dental services. He is still excited about the evolving new science in dentistry and enjoys his semi-retirement in Arizona with his wife of 40 years.

A-HA!!!!!!
SO THAT'S HOW IT ALL WORKS
Bart Gullong

I've always hated authority, and for the most part I still do. Authority in early life, childhood, adolescence, and of course, college, is about classroom education. And classroom education—although on very rare moments, interesting—for the most part, sucks.

Most classroom knowledge is controlled and presented by people who learned most of what they know from other people who spent their adult lives studying the works of other people who spent most of their adult lives pondering, studying, and learning the works of other people who spent most of their adult lives studying the works of other people, and so on.

Higher education itself is not purposely designed to prepare you for life. Instead, higher education is designed to perpetuate itself and the careers of those who are supported financially by its hallowed halls.

"Okay," you may say. "So what? I shouldn't go to college? I should go to technical school where real skills are taught?"

That answer's easy. No, because the fact is, higher education—in spite of and sometimes even because of higher educators—actually works. It works because the student, in the process of conquering the system, learns about work, pressure, process, justice, injustice, compromise, self-discipline, and most importantly, discovery.

The system simply won't admit you to the world of opportunity without that degree—that golden license to hunt.

I always felt I knew just a little better than anyone else what was good for me. I always believed that the answer, "Because I said so…" just wasn't enough to convince me. And as I progressed through school, I was seldom convinced that the "experts" teaching me, were all that expert, or in fact, were worth listening to at all.

The experts created and sustained campus rules that were totally anachronistic.

The experts got us into a war in Southeast Asia that couldn't be won.

The experts decided who, from my generation, would live and who would die with a LOTTERY!

The experts ran huge corporations that benefited financially from my generation dying in war and still do!

So I set about "discovering" my own conclusions, but I had to make it simple so I could remember it.

So I made it simple. Business is bad, hating business is good. Business is destroying the world with greed. Art, music, writing, and poetry are the only hope to save the world with good and create peace. "The system" is bad. Anything that supports the system, like business, is worse. Fighting "the system" is good.

So I got my license and off I went into the world to hunt, still hating authority and "the system" as I did from early childhood, for all the standard reasons.

I became a coach so I could change "the system" by training others to row fast? Hmmm…Well, I could train them to fight "the system" while I was training them to row fast. And I did. I preached to all my rowers to question authority at all times, just not my authority.

I hated business still. While I was coaching and running

student activities at a college, then "deaning" student life at a college (I know what you're thinking, but I wasn't in the classroom) I preached to my students to work for world peace, not business.

The Cold War was still going on, the Soviet Bloc was menacing—no end was in sight. And while I was preaching to stay out of business and fight for world peace, business did a sneaky thing. It won the Cold War—not on purpose, but then again, most great changes in the world aren't made on purpose.

The Soviets screwed up—big. They let their citizens have VCRs. They didn't realize that video tapes could be passed from hand to hand, watched, copied, and passed on again, without censorship, and suddenly Soviet citizens were able to see that life outside the USSR did, in fact, not suck as much as they were led to believe. In fact, life was a whole lot easier outside the USSR. And if history teaches us anything, it teaches us that the most powerful force in the universe is a parent wanting a better life for his or her child—and a Big Mac.

The second big mistake was the opening of a McDonald's in Moscow, lending absolute, tasteable proof that life in the free world was much better than in the USSR.

And then it all started to crumble. Slowly at first, but finally, with the speed of an avalanche, the Iron Curtain fell and, for a brief moment in time, there was world peace. And it really screwed up everything I'd come to know. It was not art, music, writing, love, and hippies singing "Kumbaya" that had brought about world peace. It was, in fact, McDONALDS!

My whole planogram was shattered.

I suddenly had to re-evaluate the impact of business—and, oh yeah, MONEY—as a major force to do good. And suddenly I learned two things. One, my entire life I had foolishly jumped to conclusions about many things, particularly doing good, and more importantly, the only way to truly fight authority is to become authority, because authority will always make the rules.

So I worked very hard to become authority, and along the way I found great people, started a couple of great businesses, the last of which has produced a product that already has saved thousands of lives by stopping bleeding on the battlefield, and soon will save hundreds of thousands more lives by stopping bleeding on the highways of the world—and, oh yeah, I made enough money to retire.

So the moral—or immoral—is, do what you have to do. Suck it up if you have to. Get your license to hunt. Find your own way. Chart your own path or follow someone else's.

But do what you have to do to BECOME authority, and then do all the good you can. Use that authority to make the planet just a little (doesn't have to be a lot), just a little bit better.

And things will work out for all of us.

of Sudden Realization, Inspiration, and Insight from 26 Professional Men

Bio of Bart Gullong

Bart Gullong grew up in Connecticut and graduated from Tabor Academy in Marion, Massachusetts. Since earning a bachelor's degree in English from Marietta College in 1970 and going on to complete a master's degree in counseling and psychology from Central Connecticut State University, Bart has enjoyed a career in business and product development, serving as a consultant to such worldwide organizations as the US and International Olympic Committees and NASA.

Bart joined On-Site Gas Systems in 1998 and was instrumental in the development of a portable oxygen generation system adapted for military use in far-forward military hospital units. Employed extensively in Iraq and Afghanistan, the systems were also used in the immediate aftermath of Hurricane Katrina in New Orleans. At On-Site, Bart discovered that his partner had invented and patented a blood-clotting element, but had been unable to effectively market the product. Recognizing an opportunity to get a valuable and potentially life-saving item into wider distribution, Bart founded Z-Medica. Developing an application that adapted the crude product for more general distribution, the product, Quikclot, is now in use by the US military as well as military organizations in a number of other countries.

Further innovation and development have yielded life-saving products for all situations where blood loss is an issue—for the soldier on the battlefield, the first responder on the scene, the doctor in the hospital, and now even the civilian at home.

Bart's recently formed Quikclot Foundation will ensure that even the poorest of countries and people will have access to this life-saving technology. He holds a 100-Ton Power and Sail All-Ocean Operators license and is the recipient of the Coast Guard Medal, the highest civilian award given by the USCG.

OF SUDDEN REALIZATION, INSPIRATION, AND INSIGHT FROM 26 PROFESSIONAL MEN

My A-ha Moments

H.E. "Doc" Holliday, Ph.D.

My personal journey of becoming a young man and automatically assuming the responsibilities that go with that role started during my early adolescent years. I grew up in the 1950s and '60s in the segregated North, in Dayton, Ohio. While there were many perceived drawbacks to this way of life, it did offer many advantages. There was a strong Triad in place within each community that consisted of open lines of communication between the home, the church, and the school. Just about everything revolved around those three entities and there was no mistaken what your role as a child was. You were expected to go to school, get good grades, get involved in activities or sports, stay out of trouble, and treat your elders with respect. There was no room for negotiation when discussing any component of this ironclad Triad. You either followed the rules or suffered the consequences. There was no in between! Most young people were hungry for success and worked diligently toward personal and community goals. Community success stories were identified and celebrated in the home, school, and church. Most of the local communities supported its collective overall success. This meant that many hard working adults took great satisfaction in seeing entire groups of young people make good on their promise to be exceptional citizens of color whether they were related to each other or not.

I grew up understanding that presenting anything less than

my best work would be unacceptable. This theme has guided my thinking for my entire life. Most young people crave to be a part of something wholesome and worthwhile. During the 1950s and '60s, there was a preponderance of positive experiences that you could gravitate to. Both of my parents were recent transplants from the Deep South and had migrated to Ohio to secure a better way of life. They both embraced the significance of attaining a quality education. This belief was instilled in my siblings at a very early age. They encouraged us all to participate in athletics, but only if we maintained an A/B grade point average. This was nonnegotiable! We had parameters and boundaries and roles set for us at a very early age. People today would characterize them as core values to live by.

The first core value centered on attaining a quality education. I was exposed to this concept because both of my parents were denied the opportunity to earn a high school diploma while living in the state of Georgia.

We had a large extended family on both my mother's and my father's side. My relatives in the Deep South were transitioning, just as we were up in Ohio, but they had a much more difficult challenge on their hands with Jim Crow laws and outright segregationist laws. We would visit our relatives during each summer to reconnect and keep abreast of family members and the latest conditions of living in the Deep South. I developed a new appreciation for the high quality educational program I was receiving in Ohio after visiting rural Georgia. I still loved traveling down South because I had so many uncles and older male cousins to emulate and learn from. My father had seven brothers and my mother had nine brothers. I must admit that I did not take all of their advice, but there was enough good information shared with me that I really had a lot to think about once I traveled back in Ohio.

Many of my uncles helped me to understand the tremendous opportunities that were afforded to me just by living in the North during this period of time in the US. They emphasized, along with my parents, that getting a quality education was not always possible while living in the segregated South. They helped me to realize that this was one of the primary reasons that my parents had made the very difficult transition of moving to Ohio even when the vast majority of their families had remained in the South. I now had a real sense of purpose that would help guide my thinking in all of the years that have come and gone since those days. All of my uncles said that it would not be easy, but I had an obligation to use my intellectual talents and reach for the stars whenever it came to getting a good education and positively addressing new challenges in life. They all cautioned me to never be afraid of failure because good preparation and hard, smart work would be more than an equalizer. The other lesson that I learned from my relatives in the South was that several of them had earned a college degree during the 1950s and early 1960s. I had good role models to learn from, and I did!

I took many of these new lessons home to Ohio and put them into practice. I now better understood the value of attaining a quality education and I, like so many others of my Dayton, Ohio, peers at this time, put our collective noses to the grindstone and excelled academically and athletically. We became model students who excelled in many areas while attending high school. We were leaders when it came to setting examples and reaching new heights and new goals. Failure was not an option. Through positive peer pressure, most of the 400–500 students who graduated from my high school went on to college. That was an expectation and besides no one really looked forward to joining the military to fight in Vietnam. That was an extra incentive to matriculate to a university campus.

I was the first of my family in Ohio to graduate from a four-year college. I am proud to claim to be the first because that is an honor that will be associated with me forever. I had the responsibility not only to begin college, but there was the sobering expectation to complete that degree in a timely manner. The entire family was depending on me to be a good example for others to emulate. As one of the older children in my family, I was always expected to set a good example for the others, even when the proverbial bar was always set extremely high. You had a responsibility to dig down deep and put in the work necessary to become successful. Failure was never a consideration! You performed at a high level even when the odds were against you. My father had a saying: "You can do anything in life you set your mind to do if you really want to." I was taught to depend on my own talents and efforts if I wanted to get ahead in life. I was taught to be confident in knowing that I was well prepared to face even the most overwhelming challenges in life. This advice has continued to resonate with me ever since I was old enough to acknowledge my father's timely advice. I also adhered to a song that the Godfather of Soul, James Brown, once sang, "You don't have to give me nothing, just open up the door and I will get it myself." I became self-reliant and depended on my God-given talents to carve out a good life.

Throughout the years, I have tried to model my behavior after the most successful men I had come into contact with. These men did not always look like me or even grow up in the same environment that I was most familiar with. These men did have a basic code of beliefs, attitudes, and behaviors that governed their life. I just naturally became attached to these concepts as well. I have identified these ideas as values that many successful men knew and embraced. It did not matter where you lived or how much money your family accumulated. There were a set of "core values worth knowing" that many men built their lives around. You could really tell if you were in the company of men who really did not understand or believe in these concepts. They seemed to have a different moral compass that guided their very existence.

The following are time-tested core values that every young man should become familiar with:

1. The importance of attaining a quality education
2. The importance of family and true friends
3. The importance of a strong work ethic

OF SUDDEN REALIZATION, INSPIRATION, AND INSIGHT FROM 26 PROFESSIONAL MEN

4. The importance of treating women with respect and dignity
5. The importance of delaying immediate gratification and planning for the future
6. The importance of respecting adults and authority
7. The importance of having a strong personal spiritual base
8. The importance of looking and acting like you are "about something"
9. The importance of learning to work with both your hands and your mind
10. The importance of networking in the community at large
11. The importance of joining an organization or sports team (no man is an island)
12. The importance of maintaining your poise while under pressure
13. The importance of saving for a rainy day
14. The importance of always striving for excellence in everything that you do
15. The importance of being physically fit
16. The importance of pursuing self-actualization (Maslow's Theory)
17. The importance of freeing your mind from hatred
18. The importance of giving more than you receive and always helping others
19. The importance of thinking with a positive outlook
20. The importance of fearing/respecting someone or something
21. The importance of setting personal goals
22. The importance of being humble and "walking softly but carrying a big stick"
23. The importance of developing your personal "man-tra"/vision
24. The importance of reading and listening between the lines
25. The importance of moving from poverty thinking to middle-class thinking
26. The importance of being well read and informed
27. The importance of being twice as good and twice as prepared

as your competition
28. The importance of developing self-discipline
29. The importance of understanding and embracing technology
30. The importance of maintaining balance in your life

There is a growing disconnect between the real world and the perceived world of 21st century boys. It really does not matter whether you were taught by your father, grandfather, uncle, cousin, or any other responsible male who felt it was important to pass along these words of wisdom.

There has been a dramatic disconnect in the delivery of this information, especially with the disruption of the American family structure, the dramatically increased numbers in single mothers raising 21st century sons, and the dramatic increase in the number of divorces in the US. My new role has evolved from one who has benefited from having been exposed to the great teachings of countless selfless, generous, experienced men to one who can and must share knowledge and expertise to help shape the lives of young males throughout our great nation. There must be a systematic approach from like-minded men who have now drawn a line in the proverbial sand to say that we will no longer tolerate the senseless disorder that currently engulfs and negatively consumes the lives of far too many young men in America.

As I look back and reflect on my life, I want to be able to give back some of the good ideas, beliefs, and energy that I so readily received. 21st century males have much different attitudes than the ones in my generation. Today's young men are much less patient and have been conditioned to generally pursue things that offer immediate gratification. I do not think that these young men desperately want to establish a positive relationship with a well-intentioned adult. They seek positive feedback and want to be a part of a winning team or program. These are some of the attributes and beliefs that helped guide my own life as a young man.

I have written several books chronicling the plight of boys. My most recent book is *Reconnecting, Redirecting & Redefining*

OF SUDDEN REALIZATION, INSPIRATION, AND INSIGHT FROM 26 PROFESSIONAL MEN

21st Century Males (Roman Littlefield Publishers). I have this fundamental belief that the vast majority of young men do not start out wanting to fail in life. On the contrary, they desperately want to succeed but lack positive role models to help them navigate the many decisions and choices that always seem to crop up and complicate their lives. It is my heartfelt belief that the development of a systematic approach to share the wisdom of many well-intentioned males would be a tremendous step in the right direction. This gesture will at least ensure that all males are working off the same page and enlisting expecting America's elders to step up to the plate, get directly involved, and finally "put some skin in the game."

Bio of Dr. Earl Holliday

H. E. "Doc" Holliday has retired from a tenured associate professor in the Department of Educational Leadership at Kennesaw State University after serving as the principal of Campbell Middle School in Cobb County, Georgia. He received his PhD from Ohio State University, a master's in education from Kent State University (Ohio), and a BA from Marietta College (Ohio). The former Assistant Superintendent for School Improvement in the Cobb County School District, as well as the Chief of Staff in the Atlanta Public School, Dr. Holliday is a frequent presenter at national, regional, and statewide conferences. He has previously instructed at KSU and Ohio State University. He has served as a building principal in four different decades in both Georgia and Ohio. He has experience in urban, suburban, and rural districts. He has given lectures and workshops in Brazil, Mexico, and China.

Dr. Holliday's schools have always been characterized by high expectations, a diverse population, innovative programs, and high academic achievement. His schools have produced over 94 National Merit Finalists, 25 National Achievement Finalists, 45 Commended Merit students, and 15 Commended Achievement students. He has crafted a reputation as a strong academician. One example is, while principal of Wheeler High School in Cobb County, Georgia, he raised the SAT scores 43 points in just three years by creating an Academic Booster Club and a school Renaissance Program (student academic incentive program).

Dr. Holliday has always been on the cutting edge of innovative educational programs while leading challenging local schools. During the past five years, he has successfully developed a number of programs for at-risk students. He has recently been engaged in developing a series of Mother/Son Parental Engagement workshops. He developed an interactive, web-based survey (found at www.edtransform.com) to gather attitudinal data on males. He introduced an innovative gender-based education program (separation of boys and girls classes) with a great deal of fanfare in 2003. His school test scores took dramatic double-digit gains for all ethnic groups, and he became a speaker in great demand. He also introduced mandatory school uniforms, curriculum mapping, and a movement from block scheduling back to traditional scheduling.

Dr. Holliday's first book, *Gender Education in 7 Steps: Reigniting the Academic Pilot Lights of Boys and Girls*, was published in 2007. His second book is appropriately titled *Boys: Transitioning from Athletic Aggression to Academic Affirmation* was published in the summer of 2009. His third book was *Reconnecting, Redirecting, and Redefining 21st Century Males*. It was designed to provide common-sense solutions for American public schools when engaging boys and discouraging them from dropping out of school. Dr. Holliday just completed his first children's book entitled *Core Values Worth Knowing: From a Third Grade Point of View*.

Dr. Holliday has been teaching a variety of classes while on the Kennesaw State University campus. He was invited to serve on the Ohio Governor's Task Force on Closing the Achievement Gap of African American Males. He has a strong interest in curriculum, instruction, and urban leadership development, and he is interested in connecting the theories generated by university professors with the real-world, day-to-day challenges at the local school level. For more information, go to Google and search for "H.E. 'Doc' Holliday, PhD".

Contact Information

H.E. "Doc" Holliday, PhD
932 Village Greene NW
Marietta, Georgia 30064

hhollida@kennesaw.edu
www.boystransitioning.org
www.gendereducation.net

OF SUDDEN REALIZATION, INSPIRATION, AND INSIGHT FROM 26 PROFESSIONAL MEN

The Heart of the Decision
Earle Maiman

The events that gave rise to my *A-ha Moment* occurred in 1969.

Although the '60s are often looked back upon with some nostalgia through the gauzy haze of time, the fact is that those were very turbulent years in which many horrific events occurred.

The world literally teetered on the edge of nuclear war in 1962 when the United States and Russia had a blood-chilling stare-down over missiles based in Cuba. In 1963, civil rights leader Medgar Evers was shot and killed. Also in 1963, President John F. Kennedy was shot and killed. In 1965, Malcolm X was shot and killed. In 1968, Martin Luther King was shot and killed. Also in 1968, Robert F. Kennedy was shot and killed.

And, of course, thousands upon thousands of America's young men were shot and killed—or killed in many other horrible ways—in Vietnam, a small nation in Southeast Asia that plainly was of no genuine strategic significance whatsoever to the United States. By the end of the war in Vietnam, more than 58,200 young Americans had lost their lives for no good reason. Over 300,000 were wounded in the war, 75,000 of whom were listed as "severely disabled."

The war in Vietnam was made even worse by the fact that a substantial number of soldiers sent into that combat were serving against their will. Over 1,700,000 young men were drafted into the military. Over 30% of all combat deaths were suffered by soldiers who had been forced into service by the government.

At home, blood literally ran in the streets of America's cities as young people protested the war, and as blacks and other minorities struggled to achieve basic civil rights and the benefits of equal opportunity.

Thus, although there were plenty of good times with great music, recreational drugs, and so-called "free sex" in the '60s, the truth remains that many people suffered terribly during those years.

I was one of the lucky ones. I came from a home with adequate resources to afford a higher education and I enrolled at a seemingly idyllic school in southeastern Ohio called Marietta College. Under the rules then in effect, I was exempted from the draft for as long as I was a full-time student in college. In truth, I was genuinely interested in continuing my education and sincerely wanted to do well at school. However, I was also acutely aware that my college enrollment insulated me from the draft and from the probability of being shipped off to do battle in the rice paddies of Vietnam. Simply put, I was horrified at the prospect of being killed or disabled in a war that was so manifestly unjustified and wrong.

As things turned out, even idyllic Marietta College was not immune from the turmoil of the times. Marietta was a small place, with only 1,700 students. Many of those students were very bright, intellectually curious, and self-assured. However, despite the groundswell of progressive change sweeping the nation, the administration at Marietta insisted on treating these students as if they were feckless children. Women were required to be in their dorms by 10:00 p.m. Students who could legally drink alcohol were prohibited from doing so on campus. The administration monitored the personal lives of students, going so far as to chastise and warn those who engaged in interracial dating. Students were prohibited any meaningful role in the formulation of social rules and were likewise excluded from participation in any committees or activities that helped set the academic course of the institution. Priorities were skewed. A young man could be expelled for having a female in his room, but he would receive only a slap on the wrist for academic plagiarism. In short, although the school had many brilliant faculty members and outstanding students, Marietta operated in an environment that was repressive and stifling. Thus, while many Marietta students were vehemently opposed to the war, much of their energy was directed toward addressing conditions on campus that they found so hard to bear.

Against this background, I found myself actively involved in student government and in an effort to reform the administration's most repressive on-campus social and academic policies. At the end of my junior year, in 1969, I ran for president of the student body on a platform devoted entirely to bringing about change in the way the school was run. Essentially, I wanted the school's administration to treat students like the young adults they were, treat women and minorities with respect, and to enhance the academic quality of the school by opening avenues for greater student input and feedback.

I was elected president. The school's administration was not happy. Without a doubt, I was seen as a threat. It did not take long for the administration to do something about it.

My very first act as president of the student body was to give a speech at an event called "the President's Roundtable." This was a monthly meeting at which the president of the college and the president of the student body were each to speak about on-campus events and activities. In the past, the Roundtable had been a pretty benign event. However, I used the occasion to lay out the grievances of the student body as I perceived them and to demand that action be promptly taken to resolve those issues. It is probably worth noting that I was not wearing a tie-dyed T-shirt, cutoff jeans, buffalo-hide sandals, or a headband at the time of the speech. I was actually wearing a sports coat and tie. But I spoke from the heart—and I guess I spoke rather forcibly.

Upon the conclusion of my remarks, the president of the college stood up, announced that he resented the tone of my comments, and stormed out. Later that day, he called me to his office. I went, assuming that he had calmed down and was ready to talk about making some progress on the matters I had raised. Instead, to my shock and dismay, he handed me a letter telling me I was expelled from the college.

When the news of my expulsion got out—which took about ten minutes—the student body mobilized in remarkable ways. Students sat on the steps of the administration building blocking access. About 100 students went on a hunger strike, asserting they would not eat until I was reinstated. There were demonstrations and a casket was carried through campus announcing the death of free speech. The event became something of a media circus as well. The story was carried both nationally and internationally with much commentary on the subject of First Amendment free speech rights.

In the midst of all this, I had a terrible problem well beyond the immediate issue of being expelled from school. Notice of the expulsion reached my hometown newspaper in Pennsylvania and was picked up by the local draft board. I promptly received a notice advising me to report for military service. Vietnam loomed.

Then came the most difficult moment of all. In light of the vehement student reaction, public pressure, and a variety of other factors, Marietta's administration advised me in private that I could stay in school if I resigned my position as president of the student body. In other words, not only could I put an end to all the turmoil on campus and alleviate my parents' extreme anxiety, but I could most importantly avoid being sent to Vietnam if only I would turn my back on the issues I had spoken about at the President's Roundtable.

It was a terrible decision to make. I believed in the things that I had said. I believed I had the right to say them. Yet, at least in the short term, life would be so much easier if I simply walked away from those beliefs. But the short term is not what life is all about. Even at the age of 20, I instinctively knew that my sense of self would be forever compromised if I did what was expedient rather than doing what I knew was right. That was my *A-ha Moment*.

I turned down the administration's offer, and I will forever be at peace for having made that decision.

Things turned out okay for me. I was able to obtain a court order allowing me to stay at Marietta for the rest of the academic year. The public reaction to the administration's conduct was so intense that many of the reforms I had sought were put in place. I went on to law school, a successful career, and a terrific life with a wonderful wife and two great kids. I can't say specifically how things would have been different had I made the opposite decision that day at Marietta. But I know for sure that I would not be the person that I am today. There are some choices that go to the very heart of who someone is. Often, it is in the heart where the right decision will be made.

Bio of Earle Jay Maiman

Earle Jay Maiman is retired from the active practice of law. He lives in Cincinnati, Ohio, with his wife, Sharon, a Master Gardener and accomplished potter, and their labradoodle, Idgi, who is accomplished at being cute. Earle is the father of two sons. The elder plays lead guitar for the popular rock band Walk The Moon. The younger works in the film industry in Los Angeles.

Earle holds undergraduate degrees from both Marietta College and Ohio University, and an MA in public address from the University of Wisconsin–Milwaukee. He coached the intercollegiate debate team and taught communications at James Madison University for four years before attending law school at the University of Cincinnati.

Earle spent his entire legal career—spanning more than 30 years—with the same firm. His practice was exclusively as a trial lawyer. He primarily tried business disputes, but he also handled product liability and personal injury cases, as well as a variety of other types of contested matters. For 15 years, Earle was the head of litigation for his firm's Cincinnati office and vice-chair of the firm-wide Business Litigation Practice Group. He lectured frequently on techniques of trial practice and was chair of the Steering Committee for the National Institute of Trial Advocacy training program conducted annually at the University of Cincinnati.

Earle was listed among the "100 Best" lawyers in Ohio and "50 Best" lawyers in Cincinnati. He was the first Program Director for the Cincinnati Bar Association Arbitration Service. He is the chairman of the board of trustees for the Legal Aid Society of Greater Cincinnati. He is also a member of the Civil Service Commission of Madeira, Ohio, and he previously served on the board of that community's Historical Society.

In 2012–13, Earle was the Fitzgerald Executive-In-Residence at Marietta College, leading a program in which students could participate in a "mock" case throughout the academic year and then try the case to a jury of community members at year's end.

Unexpected Moments in an Academic Life

Charles S. Taylor, PhD

I was in first grade the first time it happened. Sitting in class one spring afternoon, we had on our desks a sheet of paper with a picture at the top and space below to practice printing letters such as "g-i-r-l," "c-a-t," or "h-o-u-s-e." While we were working on this, there was a knock at the door and our teacher invited in one of the second grade teachers who was followed by her entire class. Each student was carrying a sheet of paper with words written in cursive. They walked up and down the aisles so each of us could see what they were learning. I remember the feeling of fear I had in that moment as if it were yesterday rather than sixty years ago. I said to myself, "You will NEVER be able to do that!" It seemed wholly impossible for me to be able to write that way. It was certain that I would fail at that task. Interestingly enough, the fear seemed to disappear as suddenly as it came. I do not recall the slightest fear of inability the next year when we started to learn cursive. I seemed to have learned that task, after all, without difficulty. But the moment of feeling overwhelmed with my own inability was etched deeply in my subconscious memory and would recur infrequently.

The next time it happened was years later. By the time I had entered high school, I had grown to be of the size that meant I was expected to play football. I decided to join the team, and for several years as a younger player, I was primarily involved in practice and watching the older players perform. Through that observation, I noted a number of things about myself. Although I had grown to be six feet tall and to weigh 180 pounds, I was not particularly strong and (with my flat feet) I was decidedly slower than almost all the others on the team. Perhaps most troubling was the fact that, unlike those who were successful, I was certainly not aggressive. I also felt some fear of being injured. These observations combined to make me feel once again that I simply did not possess the required ability; I was certain I was not up to the task of being a starting player on the team. This did not pose a problem through my junior year, as there were older players who had the requisite ability. However, knowing that I might eventually be expected to play more, I embarked on a project to raise my skill level for my position at tackle. In practice, we did daily drills to improve specific actions such as keeping one's feet moving while trying to block an opposing player or keeping one's shoulders squarely aligned with one's opponent. In doing those drills, I devoted much attention to improving my skill. Others did these drills without much attention. Apparently I was a good learner. In my final year, I was always called on by coaches to demonstrate skills to the younger players. In my senior year on the team, I did end up becoming a starting offensive tackle. What I soon learned was that while I was still not as aggressive, as strong, or as quick as my opponents, I was more skilled and a "smarter" player than they were. I ended up being a far more successful player than I had ever imagined. I was not a "star" by any means, but I rose from feeling I was simply incapable of the task to realizing that I could succeed. This realization was more surprising than my having so easily learned cursive. The feeling of inability had lasted longer.

It happened again less than a year after my final football game. Although I had doubted my academic ability to learn cursive, I soon realized that I was a successful student academically and graduated at the top of my high school class. When I started college at Marietta, I had another of those episodes of fearing that I lacked the ability to succeed. Yes, I had done well in high school and on standardized tests, but I also noted that in college I was with a different group of people, all of whom had done well in high school and on those tests. Our first message from the dean of the college at our freshman convocation was, "Look to your right, look to your left. Those people will not be here in four years." He was not exaggerating. Eight hundred of us were seated at that convocation, and I graduated four years later with four hundred. But I was not thinking statistically when I feared I might not succeed. It was a much more immediate fear.

The concrete example came fairly soon. I had scored well enough on the SAT quantitative section to be placed in a calculus class in which I was the only person not to have had a year of calculus in high school. The first test was analytic geometry, and having had that in high school, I ended up with the highest grade in the class. The second exam was on a difficult concept: limits. I had the lowest score in the class. I felt lost—completely lost. For an intended science major, calculus was absolutely essential. In our calculus textbook, all the odd-numbered problems had the answers given in the back of the book. For the next test, I worked every single one of the odd-numbered problems until I got the correct answer. Somewhere in that process I finally grasped the different conceptual framework of calculus. From that point on, I never had problems understanding math. In fact, at one point my calculus teacher tried to persuade me to switch to being a math major instead of my then intended major of chemistry. "Lots of people can do chemistry. Only a few can do math. You can," he said. I ended up instead in Europe spending a year studying history, art, and politics in Vienna and then returning to earn a degree combining political science, history, and philosophy.

It was not until halfway through the first semester of my senior year of college that I finally realized that I wanted to study and teach philosophy at the university level. I applied to graduate school and with some luck was accepted into two good graduate programs, Boston College (BC) and the New School for Social Research. I soon realized that I was nowhere near as prepared for graduate study in philosophy as were all my peers at BC. Once again, I had that intermittently recurring feeling of fearing my own

ability to succeed. Once again, I noted that while I had done well in diverse subjects from calculus and chemistry to English literature and history, I certainly lacked the advanced understanding of philosophy common among the other students. I seriously questioned whether I could succeed in graduate school in philosophy.

Noting my lack of background, I decided to focus on learning the history of philosophy rather than wondering, as other new grad students did, what the topic of my dissertation would be. Fortunately, BC emphasized the history of philosophy and I was able to enroll in classes on the Pre-Socratics, Plato, Aristotle, Descartes, Kant, and Hegel early in my studies. At the end of the first year, there was a mandatory exam for all students. I initially failed that exam, but the faculty concluded that I had sufficient promise to allow me to retake the exam. I completed it the second time successfully, passed my final comprehensive exams with distinction, and completed all my degree requirements in four years. I was among the first of my class to finish. I was also the first BC grad student to have a dissertation director from Europe. I spent a year in Belgium working with a professor at the Université catholique de Louvain.

The next several years involved the struggle to find a permanent teaching position in philosophy at a university. I was fortunate enough to get one-year visiting professor positions at Creighton University and Southern Oregon State University. I finally was offered another visiting professor position that became a tenure-track position at Wright State University. It soon became clear to me that as a young, growing university, WSU's expectations for faculty success were undergoing significant changes. While successful teaching had been the defining element for faculty promotion, a record of scholarly publication was being added to the requirements. In my first year, that was made clear by the denial of tenure to a colleague in philosophy who had not published. Add to that the fact that at that time only five percent of essays submitted to philosophy journals were accepted for publication, and it might not be surprising to hear that once again I felt that feeling of fear that I would not be able to succeed in the world of publishing in philosophy. There was no doubt in my mind that, while I had completed my PhD, I was not in the upper ranks of grad students in philosophy.

Once again I doubted my own ability to compete with this new elite group of tenure-track assistant professors in philosophy. Although I do not recall making the connection, I did in fact start on a path similar to ones I had taken previously in similar situations. I had worked hard at learning basic skills in football, worked hard at solving calculus problems, and worked hard at learning the history of philosophy. And now as a young assistant professor, I began to work very hard at my scholarly writing. A big snowstorm in my first year closed the university for several days. I used the time to write and did little else. I received many rejection letters from journal editors, but I just kept writing and sending out the essays to different journals. Curiously, several ended up being published eventually by more prestigious journals than the ones I had initially tried. Often these acceptances came with little or no revision to the originals because I had not agreed with the initial reasons given by reviewers for rejection. The outcome was that I was granted tenure and subsequently promoted to the rank of professor.

Within two years of my promotion to professor, another event brought about a change in my university career. The review process for my promotion to professor had made it clear to me that I had some status among Nietzsche scholars. This encouraged me to work more on my writing. However, at the same time, I had developed a detached retina and ended up losing all the vision in my right eye. I had earlier had a detached retina in the left eye and had lost some vision in it. One might expect the outcome of these vision problems to have been another episode of my recurring fear of ability to succeed. Nothing like that happened. I realized that with my low vision, I would no longer be able to read at the volume that would allow me to continue a serious program of publication. Nor could I teach as much as I had been, because reading was an essential element to my teaching. The one option was to take on administrative tasks in place of some of my teaching load. Administration had never been my intended path in the university but it was a necessary change. I became the director of a graduate program in the humanities, then chair of (eventually) three departments: philosophy, religion, and classics.

The latest moment of fear of my ability to succeed came after six years as a department chair. The dean of our college was selected to become the dean of a much larger college, at her alma mater. In the process of selecting an interim dean, I was surprised to learn that I was under consideration. I had never imagined being dean or wanting to be dean. In the end, I agreed to become interim dean with the clear intention of not being a candidate for the permanent position. Having worked quite closely with the outgoing dean while I was a department chair, I was well aware of how different she and I were. I could imagine myself managing the internal university politics that deans must manage, but I could not imagine myself involved in fundraising or being a public figure representing the college. I hesitatingly decided to be a candidate, guided by Plato's comment that the penalty for not being willing to rule is to be ruled by someone worse than yourself. I was sure that a better candidate would be found and I would return to the quiet life of a department chair.

Well, I was appointed dean of the college. And I did once again feel that instinctive fear that I could not succeed at some important required tasks. I was certain I would have to become a different kind of person to manage the public and philanthropic aspects of the job. At the age of 57, I knew it was not likely I would or could change. I started on the same kind of path that I had taken before. I did not avoid the fearful tasks but chose to work at them despite the deep uneasiness. As I met with potential donors and made appearances representing the college, I began to realize that I could in fact "be me" and do these things. I soon found myself quite comfortable in the very situations in which I was certain I could not succeed. More than any of the other experiences related in this story, I was extremely surprised to learn how well I could do things I thought I could not do at all. As this lesson began to sink in, I started to recall the earlier versions and see the thread connecting them. We typically try to do things we have some confidence that we can do. We may even try things for which we have no sense of either success or failure. We avoid those tasks we believe we cannot do. To learn, as I did, that you can do something you were certain you could not do is a marvelous lesson. It took me a long time, but it was the best of lessons.

of Sudden Realization, Inspiration, and Insight from 26 Professional Men

Bio of Dr. Charles S. Taylor

Dr. Charles S. Taylor is dean and professor of philosophy emeritus at the College of Liberal Arts, Wright State University. Before his seven-year term as dean, Dr. Taylor served as chair of the Departments of Religion, Philosophy, and Classics for six years and director of the Master of Humanities Program for five years during his 35-year career at Wright State. Dr. Taylor chaired searches for deans of Engineering and Computer Science and for the School of Graduate Study, and he served on search committees for the provost and the Vice President for Advancement. He was chair of the University Technology Committee, the Liberal Arts Technology Committee, and the Provost's Task Force on Technology. Charitable giving to the College of Liberal Arts increased from $670,000 annually to $2 million annually while Dr. Taylor was dean.

During the first half of his career at Wright State, Dr. Taylor advanced to the rank of professor of philosophy as a specialist in modern European philosophy. Special interests included philosophy and literature and the philosophy of art. His scholarly publications explored Nietzsche, as well as Schopenhauer, Kant, Heidegger, and writers Nikos Kazantzakis, Hermann Hesse, Ernest Hemingway, and Italo Calvino. He also published essays on using technology in teaching. Dr. Taylor was the founding editor of *Mad River*, a journal of essays for the educated reader.

Dr. Taylor earned a BA from Marietta College and a PhD from Boston College. While at Wright State, he received the National Award for Innovative Teaching, Learning and Technology (1997). At Marietta College, he was elected to Omicron Delta Kappa and was awarded the E.B. Krause Chemistry Award.

Since retiring from Wright State, Dr. Taylor has begun a series of essays on fine wine and the philosophy of art. The first, "Expect the Unexpected: Heraclitus, Kant and the Aesthetics of Fine Wine," has appeared in *The World of Fine Wine*, no. 43. He mentors new deans and administrators at Wright State and serves on the board of trustees of Chamber Music in Yellow Springs.

Dr. Taylor and his wife, Kim Iconis, dwell on their microfarm, *Clos Nous*, near Yellow Springs, Ohio. They grow much of their own organic fruits and vegetables. Wanting to live as sustainably as possible, they have installed an integrated geothermal and solar system that provides all their home energy needs from renewable energy.

Listen to Your Heart
Steve Brandt

It has no vocal chords but it speaks. It has no capability to process data, memorize, or adapt by learning from past actions, yet it seems to be able to do these things. It can be broken, yet it can also be mended and even strengthened after a time. It can lead a man to take actions he might not otherwise consider or assist in the consideration of actions not previously considered.

It is the heart.

The number of times I have heard someone say, "Use your head!" cannot be counted. And while I am not saying you should not give thought before taking action, I am here to say LISTEN TO YOUR HEART.

That voice inside your head (or sometimes multiple voices!) speaks. The devil is on one shoulder saying, "Do this!" The angel is on the other shoulder saying, "No! Don't do that, do this!!" Your pulse increases as you try to weigh the pros and cons. What should I do? What should I do?

LISTEN TO YOUR HEART.

There are two events in my 65 years that come to mind to illustrate this life lesson.

The first occurred at Marietta College. I chose Marietta because of its small student body (about 1,800), a beautiful campus that I fell in love with during a pre-application visit, and the small student–faculty ratio, which gave you a chance to actually get to know the professors in a way not possible at larger schools.

Not fully knowing what I wanted to do with my life, which is not uncommon when you are eighteen, I entered as a political science major. My freshman year was average, with decent but not outstanding grades. I had the advantage of being a legacy of Tau Epsilon Phi fraternity since my stepbrother was a TEP. This gave me the privilege of attending fraternity social functions and getting to know the brothers before the formal rush period began when the two-way race was on (the race by the fraternities and sororities to get the desired freshman to agree to pledge them, and the race by the freshman to get the fraternity or sorority of their choice to select them to be a pledge). I did not know it then, but some of the strongest lifetime friendships would be my TEP brothers.

During my freshman year, I started doing a shift at the college radio station. When I toured the campus, the guide noted that students from any discipline were welcome to volunteer at the station. At that moment, something clicked inside me (my heart?) and I knew that if I attended Marietta College, I wanted to work at the station. To make a long story short, by the second semester, I was made Music Director—a title that sounded much more important than it was, but I was hooked on broadcasting. In my heart, it felt right—a good fit.

Then came sophomore year. There is something called "sophomore slump" in which, after a successful first year, the second-year student falls off of the proverbial cliff with grades following into the abyss. I have always joked that if the college had not converted to computerized grading that year, my first-semester grade point average could not be calculated by hand, since it was about five or six places TO THE RIGHT of the decimal point before a number other than zero appeared.

It was a Saturday night, and a classmate in a similar position and I had way too many beers, which only enhanced

OF SUDDEN REALIZATION, INSPIRATION, AND INSIGHT FROM 26 PROFESSIONAL MEN

our depressed state instead of bolstering our feelings. We were both ready to pack and leave campus. Seriously, it was that close to happening.

At about 2:00 a.m., we decided that we needed to talk to one of our professors, who was my advisor and who was known to partake of more than his share of the spirits, but who also had a way of relating to students that not every faculty member did. Off to his place we went, and we found him well beyond sober but ready and willing to listen.

I told the professor what was going on—how I failed at everything in sight and did not really know why I was there talking with him, but what the hell, here I was. After letting me ramble, he posed a question, "Are you in college for you or your parents?"

The answer seemed obvious that I was there for me, but to him it was also obvious that I was miserable as a political science major.

"I'm here for me."

"Then you need to change your major. It's obvious you like what you're doing at the radio station, so become a radio/TV/speech major, and also change advisors!"

It was such a simple solution. It was also where my heart was. There is, however, usually a catch.

I left for Christmas break feeling pretty good about things. I would change my major and my advisor when I registered for the spring semester and that would be that—except if my grades did not substantially improve, I was warned that I would have to leave Marietta College. I was placed on academic probation. I had one semester to get it right.

Then I told my mother and stepfather, whom I consider to be my father (my biological father passed away when I was ten years old). I'm sure the neighbors thought it was a sonic boom, but it was the explosion from my family, parents, aunt, uncles, and cousins. My God, I was turning into the same "bum" that my real father was without even realizing it. No way in hell could I go into this broadcasting thing—NO WAY! Period.

I then listened to my heart. It said, go where my heart was, which was in broadcasting.

It was a long Christmas break, but somehow everyone realized how much this meant to me and that I was being my own person and not following the father I never really knew.

I went back to Marietta College, became a radio/TV/speech major (today it's called a mass communications major), changed my advisor, and made the Dean's List—no more probation. I eventually went on to become the news director of both the college's radio and television stations and eventually ascended to the top (student) position of program director of each station with a successful career in advertising that followed my graduation.

I listened to my heart after I was told that's what I needed to do.

Event number two

I was raised in the Jewish religion, being the first male child in my family, which automatically put you on a "pedestal." I went to Hebrew school for four years and, as is the custom, had my bar mitzvah when I turned thirteen and, in the Jewish religion, became a man.

When I choose Marietta College, I noticed that the Jewish enrollment was only ten percent. This really did not concern me, since I was not going to school to enhance my religious studies nor look for a wife. I really did not care about the makeup of the student body. However, when my Grandmother (all 5 feet of her) asked me about the student body and found out it was only ten percent Jewish, she said, "You are going to date only Jewish girls, right?"

"I don't know."

"What do you mean 'you don't know'?!"

"I have no idea who I am going to date in college."

Then came the bombshell. To the grandson who could do no wrong (well—most of the time), the grandson she loved more than life itself, came this:

"If you marry out of the religion, I will consider you dead."

Just like that.

And just like that, I pretty much gave up on everything that was ingrained in me about my culture and religious heritage. Just like that.

I did marry my college sweetheart. Yes, she was one of the ten percent, but the marriage lasted only a couple of years.

Fast forward about ten years later, and I fell in love with a woman of the Presbyterian faith, who at first said she would convert to Judaism. However, once I started attending church, something happened.

Listen to your heart.

I found that by attending the Presbyterian Church, I was filling a missing void in my life. For the first time since "divorcing" myself from the Jewish faith, I was finding comfort in religion through a man who was not even a part of my religious training—Jesus Christ.

After much soul searching and many discussions with my wife and ministers, I decided to listen to my heart and was baptized the same day that my oldest son was. I have since become an ordained elder and Sunday School teacher. I did learn that in the Presbyterian faith you never give up your birthright, which is from the mother. I am technically a Presbyterian Jew, or as one of my coworkers once dubbed me, a Jewbyterian!

Listen to your heart. It has a voice. It can learn, provide memories, and teach. The good news is that if you do make a mistake, it is rare that it cannot be corrected at some point. Very little is permanent—forever. But as long as you are on this earth, so is your heart. Listen.

Bio of Steve Brandt

Steve Brandt is an advertising professional with over forty years of experience in the areas of marketing, media, and creative. He started with ABC in the Networking Planning department. From there, Steve was a network planner/buyer with some of the major Madison Avenue agencies and was the supervisor of Network and Sports Franchises for Chevrolet's advertising agency, Campbell-Ewald Agency, in Detroit, where Steve headed up all network television buys and negotiations with 35 professional sports teams. He also was a media director at several agencies in North Carolina. Before joining Fairway Outdoor Advertising in 1992, Steve headed up an in-house agency for five automotive dealerships.

The father of two boys, Sean (29) and Patrick (28), Steve has won regional and national Addy Awards for creative excellence in advertising. He also was an adjunct faculty member at Alamance Community College for nineteen years and conducted numerous small business workshops.

Steve serves on the Pleasant Garden, North Carolina, Town Council, is the secretary of the Cabarrus County Rotary Club, and is a Paul Harris +1 Fellow

My A-ha Moment
Sudden Realization, Inspiration and Insight

Ricardo Anderson, PhD

Family Background

I was born into a medium-sized family. I am the youngest of five children, with one older brother and three older sisters. There is a nine- to eighteen-year age gap between my siblings and me. So by the time I was nine or ten, all of my siblings were adults. Also during this time, I witnessed the devastation in the form of drugs, alcohol, prostitution, and violence that claimed my siblings' lives. During that time, none of my siblings had any higher education, Christianity was not a way of life for us, and all of our fathers were absent from the home and our lives. My mother had raised them and was raising me all on her own with no help from anyone. Even though my mother was an alcoholic, she still provided a level of stability for me. She kept the home clean and, even though money was tight at times, I had at least two meals per day. I got to spend a lot of quality time with my mom because all of my siblings had moved out on their own. During the quality quiet times with my mother, she would talk to me about God and she would encourage me to obtain the highest level of education I could. She said through education and God, I would gain true freedom and stability. A week before she died, she sat me down and told me that she was sorry about how our lives had been, and that she loved me, but she needed me to find God and to pursue

my education because she did not want me to travel the same path my siblings had taken. A week later I found my mother dead. I was only twelve years old.

Life with my Family

Life with my family was no walk in the park. There were fights between my mother and my siblings at times. She would drink so much sometimes, she would have seizures and I would have to take care of her. At times, some of her male friends were creeps, but nothing would prepare me for what would happen to me over the next few years of my life. The night my mother died, my father came for me. I was hurting, I had just lost my mother and my best friend, but the thought of going with my father did provide a level of safety in my mind. Little did I know I would experience everything but safety.

That night, when I got to my father's house, I was told it was late and I needed to go to bed. I was led to a bedroom where there were four young boys who were already occupying this bedroom. My father told me to go in the room and go to sleep, and he shut the door. It was dark. When I found a space in one of the beds to lie down, I crawled in still fully dressed and pushed myself to the wall. I just laid there and cried. I was not in the bed for fifteen minutes when one of the older boys began to try to sexually abuse me. I balled my body up as tight as I could, and I fought him off for hours. Eventually he left me alone. I never went to sleep that night. I cried. Quickly I would find out that living with my father would be a nightmare. He sold crack cocaine and he also used it; at times I don't even know if he knew I was even there. About a year later, my father would go to prison, and at the age of 13, I would end up running for my life from his abusive girlfriend and her sons. The night I ran, one of her sons had stabbed me. A family member picked me up walking down the street carrying a garbage bag of all that I owned. From age thirteen to fifteen, I would be shuffled from house to house, relative to relative, finding out quickly I was worth nothing more than food stamps or a government check to them. After my mother's death, all of the men in the family I had once looked up to from the outside looking in, I became part of their world. All of the black men I once thought were strong and wise were drug addicts, alcoholics, and so many other hurtful things. It made me sick; I knew I did not want to be that type of man. I was teased, talked about, and sometimes hit because I would not drink or smoke and I did not believe in violence. I was the complete opposite of the people who were my black male role models.

I had one outlet, and it was school. Not only did I love learning, but I knew that when I went to school, I would get at least two meals that day, free breakfast and free lunch. At times, I would sneak to the Boys and Girls Club to eat dinner. It provided structure, safety, and stability. At the age of sixteen, I graduated from high school, entered college, and obtained full time employment.

This was a whole new world for me, living on campus and being independent. I did not always have those two meals per day because now I had bills to pay. I was not even a legal adult yet, but I had many responsibilities. Some believe they cannot go to college if they are not extremely smart. It is not always all about being smart; with drive and determination and God, you can accomplish anything.

While at Marquette University, I obtained a bachelor's degree and something wonderful happened to me: I gave my life to Christ. God began to strategically place the right mentors in my life. One was a pastor and the others were professional educators. These men were father figures, mentors, and friends. I would go on to obtain a double master's degree and a doctoral degree. I became a fourth grade teacher while still going to college. It was more than a career—it became a passion. Just by dealing with my students and their parents, I could see that many of my students were trapped in the same type of home environment I came out of. I knew I had a responsibility to not only be someone they could look up to, but I also had a responsibility to encourage them and let them know they could still rise. I would go on to be a vice principal, principal, and college professor. During these times, I also sought after God. I wanted to be the man that God intended for me to be, not only as an educator, but as a husband and father.

Overcoming my challenges

The first thing that helped me to overcome my challenges was going back in my mind to remember the promise I had to keep to my mom about finding God and pursuing education. I kept these precious moments with my mother alive in my heart with me because she believed in me and provided the best level of stability she could. I stayed away from where I was living at that time because it was so chaotic and the environment was filled with violence, drugs, abuse, and alcohol. I did not have the basic needs; I was lost and did not have decent clothes, hygiene, or shoes. I kept saying to myself, this is not normal and something good is going to happen for me. I felt like I was not going to make it, to achieve anything, but I kept hearing my mother's voice over and over telling me "through education and God I would gain true freedom." So I forced my mind to seek out things that were not dangerous or could cause harm to myself physically and mentally. I pursued cartooning, drawing, dancing, performing, and community service through the Boys and Girls Club. My mind and my time were filled with positive activities. I became intrigued with history, particularly black history, because I really did not know a lot except for who Dr. Martin Luther King Jr. and Harriet Tubman were because we only studied them during Black History Month. Learning about and researching black history made me aware and proud of contributions we made to the world.

My Faith

A man that believes in God, and has faith, and is rooted and grounded in God has a unique perspective on life and what God requires from a man. God began to order my steps and he became the author of my soul into manhood. I began to pray for God to help me make the right decisions concerning my life. I began to read the Bible about the attributes and the conduct of a man and how to live a Christian life. I also starting going to church regularly to hear the word of God because faith comes by hearing the word of God.

As a godly man, I must provide a spiritual foundation for my family, which is crucial for me to lead my family. The foundation is for me to teach my children how to pray and to believe in God. God commands me to love and guide my sons to become God-fearing men and leaders of their families. God commands me to love my daughters so they will look to me as an example for how a man must treat and respect a woman. As a husband, the word of God tells me that my wife is my glory and I am her covering. I am to love and cherish her as Christ loves the church. We are a family of nine, including us as parents, four adult children, two teenage children, and one grandson. My wife, Marisa, and I consistently pray for guidance for our family.

Help for our Young Males

The quest to help young males has been an ongoing issue for decades. After reflecting from my journey into manhood, I believe that all young men need to seek God, who will provide them with the faith to keep pressing on during hard times. Young men need to research and understand their own cultural heritage and family background because knowing who they are will give young men a sense of belonging in this world. Young men are living in diverse situations, so I believe young men must seek positive people, places, and things which will help them grow mentally, emotionally, and spiritually. From that, young men will begin to feel the sense of stability and confidence in their mind, and then this will help guide them on a path filled with opportunities. Adult men in our churches, community, and schools need to make themselves available to help, teach, and guide our young men.

Currently

As an adult man, I felt it was important for me to go back and establish a relationship with my father. First, I knew I had to forgive, and once that came, my father and I were able to talk. There I was at age 37, crying like I was still that 13-year-old little boy he had left behind. I needed him, and I found out he needed me too. So out of this, healing was able to take place. I also begin to help my brother and sisters further their education and help their children further their education and find employment.

Currently, I am living in Indianapolis with my wife and my children. We are currently ministers in training. We are both writing books about our lives and how God brought us through. I am working as a professor and a life coach instructor, and I also work for the state. We are active in the community by hosting Stop the Violence events and Back to School events. We also enjoy feeding the homeless and witnessing to the hurting and the lost.

MY A-HA MOMENT!

I believe my *A-ha Moment* is now, as a 40-year-old man, refusing to be a statistic, not fully knowing how to become a man, but because someone believed in me and now knowing God had his hand on me the whole time. And with him and determination, I made it, in spite of the deck that was stacked against me. When we RISE as MEN, we ensure *the next generation RISES!*

Bio of Dr. Ricardo Anderson

Dr. Ricardo Anderson has over 15 years of professional experience in education and as a school administrator. Currently, Dr. Ricardo Anderson serves as an adjunct instructor for the Academy of Creative Coaching , teaches leadership and management classes for Springfield College, works as a state worker to help families get approved for government benefits, and enjoys working with for-profit and not-for profit organizations as a grant writer. Dr. Anderson actively enjoys collaborating with colleagues from all disciplines and is a life-long learner.

Dr. Anderson received his bachelor's degrees in broad field science, history (African-American), and education from Marquette University; he holds double master's degrees in organizational management from Springfield College and in educational leadership from Cardinal Stritch University, and he holds a PhD in leadership for the advancement of learning and service, also from Cardinal Stritch University. Dr. Anderson finds comfort in spending time with his wife, Marisa, and their six children.

Follow Your Passion—It Is Your Ticket to Happiness
Barry D. Shur, PhD

I was one of the lucky ones. I knew early on that I wanted to be a research scientist. In fact, I distinctly recall the moment when it occurred! I was in fifth grade. I built a very crude microscope using a kit ordered from a matchbook cover. I put a drop of pond scum on a slide, put it under the microscope and was totally blown away when I saw the microscopic life streaming before my eyes. I soon built a small laboratory under the stairs in my basement where I dissected frogs left over from a nearby biological testing laboratory. Although my parents were very supportive of my interests, my uncle, who was our family physician, had an unusually strong influence on my budding scientific career. He gave me his old dissecting instruments, medical texts, and other paraphernalia that I still own, which made me feel like a real scientist.

I mostly tinkered around in my basement lab until I came across an old copy of *Scientific American* that featured the work of Marcus Singer, a world-renowned scientist who was studying the influence of nerves on limb regeneration. In language easily understood by the layperson, or "budding scientist," he described studies in which he rerouted the sciatic nerve to the stump of an amputated forearm to test the hypothesis that the supplemental nerve supply would be sufficient to induce regeneration of the forearm. I attempted to repeat these studies in my basement laboratory with frogs I received from the medical laboratory. Although I never had any real success, I was hooked on scientific research.

I grew up in a fairly typical middle-class home that had its share of challenges, both financial and emotional. My father's plumbing and heating business was frequently going bankrupt, with repossessors showing up at our home in the middle of the night. My mother lived a life full of frustration and guilt; frustration due to an emotionally abusive father who prevented her from taking advantage of scholarships to pursue her artistic talents, and guilt due to giving birth to my severely handicapped younger brother, Eric, for which, of course, she had no reason to feel responsible. Rightfully so, Eric's care has been the focus of my family's energies ever since. Being "lost" in my basement laboratory was my escape from the emotional and financial stresses of the home.

As soon as I entered Marietta College, a small liberal arts college in Ohio with a well-regarded science curriculum, I started pestering my advisor for access to a laboratory where I could continue my studies in frog limb regeneration. He chuckled and said I would have to wait in line behind the upperclassmen who were also looking for lab experience to enrich their medical school applications. Once he realized I wanted to be a scientist and had no interest in going to medical school, he offered me his own laboratory space, which I occupied for the remaining three years of my undergraduate studies.

Just tinkering in a lab was not going to get me into graduate school; excellent grades were needed as well. Fortunately, my fiancée relocated to Marietta College for our junior and senior years; she was the "smart" one and long ago mastered how to excel in classroom work and testing. Once she saw how poorly I prepared for courses that were of little interest to me, she sat me right back down and said, "We are just beginning to study tonight...buckle down and get serious." Despite our families' concerns that being together would cause both of our academic records to deteriorate, my fiancée's support (and expectations) resulted in my GPA rising to a near perfect A average at a time when I was taking the most demanding bioscience courses. Due to my fiancée's influence, we both graduated with honors and went off to premier institutions for graduate studies.

I knew I wanted to go to the Johns Hopkins University for my doctoral work. But, despite my good academic record, I assumed I would not be competitive with the many Ivy League applicants. I called Hopkins and asked for an interview. They said they did not need one, which I interpreted as a lack of interest in my application. So, I pressed them and asked to be interviewed anyway. I intended to "get on my hands and knees" if necessary and plead for an opportunity to be enrolled in their doctoral program. Once I arrived, the faculty director of admissions said I should speak to another faculty member, and then another, and another. I was convinced no one wanted to spend any time with me and were shuttling me off to another faculty member at their soonest convenience. After three or four hours of this, I made it back to the director of admissions, and said all I really wanted to do was to tell them that this is something I have always wanted, since fifth grade, that my life's dream was to be a research scientist. He asked if I had received their letter yet, which I had not, and told me that I was already accepted with a full scholarship and living stipend! What, you mean that an interview was unnecessary as I was already accepted? Plus, you are actually going to pay me to study and do research? I could not believe it—it was a dream come true.

Soon thereafter, all new students received a listing of the incoming class, at which time I realized I might be in over my head, as most of my classmates were coming from prestigious Ivy League institutions. How did I ever think that I could compete with these students? Nevertheless, my love of science prevailed, and I was the second in my class to graduate. Interestingly, of the approximately 25 students who entered the doctoral program with me, less than five have had successful independent scientific careers. This was the first of many times when I realized that being the smartest was not necessary to be successful in science, but being passionate about your work is.

In virtually all life science doctoral programs, students do one or more laboratory rotations to survey potential thesis mentors and research projects. At Hopkins, you were required to complete two semester-long rotations, the first one of your choosing and the second assigned by the faculty to a laboratory as far removed from your primary interest as possible (to broaden your horizons). For my first semester rotation, I chose the newest faculty member; a recently hired young hotshot who was studying embryonic morphogenesis. This was my first formal exposure to a real research laboratory, and I loved every second of it.

For my second rotation, I was assigned to a biophysics professor who was infamous among the students for dismissing my classmate from the program after he failed to complete anything of value during his first semester rotation. The student claimed he had no guidance during his rotation, as the faculty advisor was frequently out of town on business trips. When I was assigned to the same laboratory, my classmates gave me their condolences, fearing I might suffer the same fate! I was given the same project assigned to the first student and did not see my advisor again until the end of the semester, when he asked for my notebook. A few weeks later, I received a phone call to come down to his office. I had no idea why I was being called to his office and feared the same fate as my classmate, only to be given a copy of a manuscript that reported the results of my laboratory rotation project. Not only was I not expelled, but also I got my first publication from the rotation. I was on cloud nine! After five years there, I left Hopkins with my PhD and a few first-authored publications from my thesis. Apparently the work was good enough to receive a Helen Hay Whitney Postdoctoral Fellowship, of which approximately 10 are awarded nationally each year.

My love of science has guided me throughout my career, during good times as well as bad. Sure, it was tough to be on the receiving end of critical grant and manuscript reviews, but I had to learn how to "suck it up" and keep on plugging away. It took me a few attempts to receive my first federal grant to support my research project, but during these difficult times, I never thought of leaving science. I just thought I might need to look for a different venue in which to fulfill my dreams. Nevertheless, the funding did come, and my fledging career was off and running.

One of the great joys of being a research scientist in a university setting is the ability to mentor predoctoral and postdoctoral students—to share your passion for research and guide them as they launch their own careers. I have had the pleasure of mentoring 38 trainees, all of whom are now gainfully employed in some aspect of biomedical science, whether in full-time university teaching, research in a university or biotech environment, intellectual property, national science policy forums, or similar positions.

Since federal funding has fallen to historically low levels, many think there are no jobs for those entering biomedical research. Similarly, academic disciplines that rely on private foundations to support their scholarship have an even harder set of circumstances that could demoralize any young scholar newly out on his or her own. Not to worry! As dean of the Graduate School at the University of Colorado–Denver, I had the opportunity to speak to thousands of students, many of whom feared that limited job opportunities would prevent them from realizing their dreams. While not belittling the realities of the current job market, I repeatedly emphasized that despite the limited prospects and federal funds to support research, there will always be jobs and research support for talented people. I told them that immersing yourself in your passion—to lose yourself in this awe-inspiring marvel we call research and creative scholarship—is to be one of the lucky ones.

You will experience unbelievable highs when you realize that you are on to something novel, something no one has appreciated before, as well as the inevitable lows when you feel that you are not making any progress. But in the end, you—and no one else—will push the envelope further. You will persevere because of your passion; without it you will struggle. Never lose or bury your love of learning, or your passion for your chosen discipline. During my 40 years as a research scientist, I learned that despite the horrendous funding levels to support research and scholarship, despite the nit-picky reviewers' comments, despite the extremely high expectation to publish work in the leading journals, none of these issues can dampen my love of science and of creative scholarship, nor should it dampen yours.

Bio of Dr. Barry Shur

Dr. Barry Shur retired in July 2014 from his position as founding dean of the Graduate School at the University of Colorado Anschutz Medical Campus (CU Denver). There, he was responsible for building an independent graduate school to oversee around 4,000 masters and doctoral students matriculating in the 12 schools and colleges that comprise CU Denver.

Dr. Shur earned his BS degree with honors from Marietta College and his PhD from the Johns Hopkins University, and was a Helen Hay Whitney Postdoctoral Fellow at the Memorial Sloan-Kettering Cancer Center. His first faculty position was as an assistant professor of anatomy and cell biology at the University of Connecticut Health Science Center, where he was promoted to associate professor with tenure and subsequently relocated to the University of Texas MD Anderson Cancer Center in Houston as associate professor of biochemistry and molecular biology. At MD Anderson, he rose to full professor and served as interim chair of the department before relocating to the Emory University School of Medicine as the Charles Howard Candler Chair and Professor of the Department of Cell Biology. During his 14 years as chair, Dr. Shur recruited 12 tenure-track faculty, moved the department into totally new research facilities, and reorganized the educational and enrichment activities of the Department.

Dr. Shur has served as program director for two different National Institutes of Health (NIH)-funded training programs, the latter of which was featured on the National Institute of General Medical Sciences (NIGMS) website as a model program for the recruitment and training of underrepresented minority students. Dr. Shur maintained an NIH-funded research program that examined the molecular basis of mammalian fertilization and embryonic morphogenesis. He has trained 16 predoctoral and 22 postdoctoral fellows whose work has appeared in 138 publications, as well as two patents. Dr. Shur has served on multiple NIH study sections, including the Biomedical Research and Training Review Group; as external reviewer for the NIH Graduate Partnerships Program, multiple departments, and other graduate programs; and on seven editorial boards. Dr. Shur has organized a number of international symposia and has been an invited speaker at over 155 institutions and meetings. In recognition of his achievements, Dr. Shur was elected as Fellow of the American Association for the Advancement of Science in 2008.

Dr. Shur has been married for more than 43 years to his high-school sweetheart, Judith Wishna. Their daughter, Emily Shur, is a professional freelance photographer in Los Angeles, California, and is married to Isac Walter, originally from Sacramento, California.

of Sudden Realization, Inspiration, and Insight from 26 Professional Men

My A-ha Moments
Timothy Creel, MBA, MS

My definition of an *A-ha Moment* is that moment in life where a person learns something about themselves that they can apply to their future. These are moments and events that make a difference and build character and substance in a person. They are the times and happenings that turn individuals into the person they are to be in life. In my life, the vast majority of my *A-ha Moments* came from my relationship with God, my family, and sports.

I was born in Nashville, Tennessee, but lived in many places growing up including Arkansas, Hawaii, and California. My best memories of my childhood come from living on a farm in a rural community just outside of Murfreesboro, Tennessee, near Nashville. The town of Lascassas, Tennessee, was an exciting town with three general stores, a post office, and four churches. I was an only child and lived with my parents on an 80-acre farm. We raised hogs, had a large garden and fruit trees, and even had some calves on occasion. There were many large pastures in which to make my own baseball field, so there were several places to hit baseballs. It was a good life and I had a great time living there.

My family taught me so many things that belong among my *A-ha Moments*, including my work ethic and how to play sports, and they even helped me develop a relationship with God. My father had his own construction business and my mother was a homemaker who worked various part-time jobs from time to time. I owe so much to them from the way they raised me and the examples they set for me about how to become a man.

One of my earliest *A-ha Moments* came from working on the farm, as it taught me an important element, which is the importance of hard work and responsibility. There was always work to be done on the farm, as there were so many responsibilities that needed to be taken care of on a regular basis. As a kid, I raised hogs and pigs, who had to be fed twice a day. I would get up before 5:30 every morning to bottle-feed calves and feed the hogs before catching the bus to school. When I came home from school, they had to be fed again. Rain or shine, hot or cold, they had to be fed every morning and every evening.

This *A-ha Moment*, demonstrated to me by my parents, was that there are responsibilities that we must take care of and that hard work is important. These responsibilities have to be taken care regardless of the situation or difficulty in completing them. Hard work is not a bad thing, and being able to meet that challenge is a trait that an individual should have to be successful in life. These are traits that helped me in college as I went off to school and had to work hard to graduate with honors with an accounting degree. These are traits that helped me start my career as an accountant with Pennzoil in Houston, Texas, and even later to return to school to complete two master's degrees while still working full-time in accounting and education. These traits have helped me as I work to complete my doctorate in accounting (I should finish in the next few months). In addition to stressing the importance of knowing and having a relationship with God and your family, this was a very important *A-ha Moment* I learned from my parents in my youth.

My parents also encouraged me to play sports growing up, and I played baseball, softball, basketball, and football. Playing sports created many *A-ha Moments* for me through the years. One of the greatest lessons was about teamwork, since you played on a team with other individuals and you all tried to work together to achieve a purpose which was to win. I learned you had to trust your teammates to do their job. For example, when a ball was hit to me at shortstop and there was a runner on first, I had to trust that the second baseman would cover the bag for the force-out or to try and turn the double play. Communication was also very important, since the shortstop and second baseman had to communicate as to who was covering the base in case of a steal attempt by the base runner. Both trust and communication were important elements of every team sport that I played, and they taught life lessons that can be applied to the workplace, especially when I was a financial manager, or even in a family environment at home.

Perhaps the biggest *A-ha Moment* from playing sports was related to both learning how to win and how to respond positively to losing. One of my early memories of sports was playing county league softball in Lascassas, Tennessee. I was 12 years old and played shortstop, and we won the championship that year in my first year. We also won the county league championship the next year and also two years later. We won many games, and it was always fun to win. I also played high school basketball and baseball for Middle Tennessee Christian School in Murfreesboro, Tennessee, and we won about eight or nine games in my three years of playing baseball and one game in my one year of playing basketball. We did improve in baseball, as we won five or six games in my senior year.

But winning was not the best thing about playing these sports. The most fun thing was the competition and the fun I had with my teammates as we competed to win every game. When we won, we had quite a celebration, but I learned a lesson in that you do not have to win to enjoy yourself when playing sports.

The life lessons from this *A-ha Moment* were to always strive to win and to always bring your best to the game. It is a good thing to want to win every game and get a hit during every at-bat. This type of drive to win will help an individual improve and stay at the top of their game in all aspects of life, whether in sports, work, or education. I had this drive where I wanted to succeed at everything. This is a good thing, but the lesson I learned was not to let the drive to win take away from your joy and the fun you can have just from the competition. I applied this when I was in college, as a part of me wanted to work to get an "A" in every course, but I enjoyed college so much more due to the fact I balanced studying and doing fun things with friends. I still managed to graduate with honors and got a great job right out of college. I cannot remember a single test from college, but what I do remember are the fun times I had with friends.

My most important *A-ha Moment* came from deciding to become a Christian when I was a junior in high school. God had always been in my life, as I had attended church and a Christian school, but I had never made a commitment to him. Everything in my Bible classes at school just started to make sense to me and I realized that I was ready to make that commitment. I decided to be baptized after church services on a Wednesday night in October 1983. It was so important that I did it on a night during a World Series game which was pretty big since I was a huge baseball fan. My parents took me to the Lascassas Church of Christ, since they had a baptistery, while my church, the Milton Church of Christ, did not. Our minister met us there and asked me if I was ready to follow Jesus, and I said yes. He then proceeded to immerse me into the water to baptize me. There was such as feeling of joy and freedom as I made my confession and was baptized that night. My sins were washed away and I was ready to start a new life following Jesus. It was the greatest *A-ha Moment* I have ever experienced.

Becoming a Christian did not mean that life would be easy, but it did mean that he would be there to lead and guide me through his spirit. It also meant that even though I was not perfect and made mistakes, I was forgiven due to the sacrifice of Jesus. I had so much to learn after being baptized that night in October 1983, but I knew that he would be with me every step along the way. This decision helped lead me to attend Harding University in Searcy, Arkansas, and meet so many great Christian examples, both fellow students and professors. The decision to become a Christian in my junior year helped me to meet a new transfer student named Kelly Young, who I would marry about three years later. It helped me enjoy 21 great years of marriage with her as we had two sons together, Heath and Joshua. My faith also helped me when she suddenly passed away in 2011 because I would not have been able to make it without having God in my life. Even in the great tragedy of her loss, there was peace in my soul as I knew she was in Heaven celebrating with Jesus, and God blessed me with tremendous support from my family, friends, and my church. He recently led a new person into my life, Kathy Greene, and I married a beautiful, Christian woman who has helped me so much the past two years. My boys and I are part of a family again. Through both the best of times and the greatest challenges I have ever faced, God has always been there for me and I have never regretted for one moment my decision to follow him that night in October 1983. One of my favorite scriptures truly demonstrates how I feel about my relationship with God.

"For I am convinced that neither death nor life, neither angels nor demons, neither the present nor the future, nor any powers, neither the depth, nor anything else in all creation, will be able to separate us from the love of God that is in Christ Jesus our Lord."

(Romans 8:38, NIV version)

My *A-ha moments* in life come from my experiences with my family, sports, and my Christian faith. These are the moment that define a person and make them into the individual they will be in life. They are the events and instances that shape us so we can face future challenges and attain great achievements. My parents taught me so much about working hard and responsibility due to my growing up on a farm. Participation in sports taught me about winning and losing. I learned that I should always strive to win, but make sure I enjoy myself along the way. My baptism and commitment to Jesus stands out as my most important *A-ha Moment*, as it was there that I said I would do my best to follow him. All of these *A-ha Moments* have lead me to become a better person, a better father and husband, and a better educator and professional, and they have helped me to realize how blessed my life has been.

Bio of Tim Creel

My name is Tim Creel and I live in Murfreesboro, Tennessee. I work as a university professor for Tennessee State University and Strayer University, teaching accounting courses. I earned a bachelor's degree in accounting from Harding University in Searcy, Arkansas, an MBA from Lipscomb University in Nashville, Tennessee, and a master of science in accounting from Strayer University online. I am currently working on my doctorate in business administration from Nova Southeastern University in Ft. Lauderdale, Florida, and I hope to finish by the end of 2014. After the loss of my first wife, Kelly, I recently remarried, to a wonderful Christian woman named Kathy, and I have two sons, Heath and Joshua, and a stepson, Franklin. My hobbies include golf and running, and I enjoy running three or four half-marathons a year.

The Resilient Life
Dr. Wayne Norton

Kris Carr has said, "We always have the potential to rise. Rise out of our slump. Rise out of our negative thoughts. Rise out of our comfort zone. Rise out of our complaints. Get up and rise. Rising is a choice that's one powerful thought away." Resilience is a secret to a victorious voyage of life. My life story may not be impressive, but I hope I can leave a breath of fresh air about anyone's circumstances. A lady was down, discouraged, defeated, and disheartened. Someone asked her, "How are you doing?" She replied, "Very well, under the circumstances." Her listener smiled and said, "What are you doing under those?" We can have our circumstances or our circumstances can have us. The choice is absolutely ours.

For me, life has not been one of those smooth sailing trips that some people make. I am so glad! I am so thankful! I am so blessed! Why? The journey of my life may not be called a "joy ride," but through my walk with Jesus Christ, my life has become a "ride of joy." Life will have ups and downs. Some of life's ups get people into awesome places. Some of life's downs get people into awful places. Please remember that life is not about what happens to us. Life is about what happens through us!

For me, life began by being an unwanted child whose biological parents had rejected him. By the providence of God, my biological parents did not choose the route of abortion. They, instead, just abandoned me. Then a neighbor learned about this, found me, reported me to Family Services, and I was immediately hospitalized as a malnourished baby not expected to live. By the grace and providence of God, by the help of a wonderful and caring physician in that small Kansas town, and by the open door to my adoptive parents, God began to work. My adoption legally caused my adoptive parents to sell a well-established business in Cherryvale, Kansas, and make the move to Springfield, Missouri.

That was just one of innumerable sacrifices that Charles H. and Pearl M. Norton made on my behalf. From Springfield, we later moved to Mound Valley, Kansas, where I spent time in first through third grades. Then, as my father was employed at another position with Kansas State University's Experimental Farm in rural Mound Valley, another chapter opened and my years on the farm resumed from those earlier years in the Springfield area. In addition to my sacrifices, I attended a two-room elementary school in that area. These are examples of some of the greatest years of my life, preceding my father's employment with the *Coffeyville Journal* in nearby Coffeyville, Kansas. Another move opened another chapter, which allowed me to finish my senior year at Labette County High School in Altamont, Kansas, in the spring of 1966. My father was a hard worker, not a quitter. He modeled endurance, good people skills, excellent sales abilities, wisdom, resilience, and many other valuable traits. My mother also worked hard in every job that she had. Both parents taught me valuable tools that I would use to enter the workforce.

At the age of sixteen, I was approaching my junior year in high school. My boyhood dream was to be a major league baseball player. Had my abilities matched my desires, that dream might have been more realistic. That summer, I was playing ball and suffered an injury that, for all practical purposes, shattered my dream. I sat at home with a bad knee and was just becoming able to walk without help when some boys from our church approached me about going to camp. Although I was reluctant at first, they said the right words and convinced me to go. At camp, I was in trouble on the first day, but persuaded the boys' director to let me stay. He reluctantly agreed.

Then, on the next day, my being raised in a very prejudiced environment came to the surface as I walked into the room for

Bible study and met an African-American senior adult woman. She spent that session talking about God's love. Since I had just learned from my parents about my adoption, I really was not feeling loved. Angry, bitter, rejected, and totally "turned off" on religion, I sat, obviously inattentive, until Mrs. McIntosh looked directly at me, smiled with a beautiful smile, and sweetly said, "Wayne, God loves you, too." That broke the rock wall around me, softened my heart, and touched me because the Holy Spirit was working through her to convict me of my sins and to convince me of my need for Jesus Christ as my personal Lord and Savior. Every day, I became closer to this woman that my prejudicial society had taught me to hate and reject. I even interacted with the group. On that Wednesday evening, after a stirring spiritual message about salvation and a candle-light service, I sought a pastor, Rev. Vincent Hall. He was a close friend of my father's who pastored in a nearby town. Rev. Hall presented to me the plan of salvation. That night, I became forever a child of Jesus Christ. My prejudice melted under the blood of Jesus and his forgiveness. Every one of my sins were gone! I was free! I was excited! I was so happy and joyous! Jesus was alive in me!

After finding Jesus as my Savior, the next person that I found that night was Mrs. McIntosh. I threw my arms around her with love flowing from my former hate-filled heart. I asked her to forgive me for my prejudice and hatred. I told her that I was so sorry for how I had acted. She was so happy and said to me, "Wayne, I can see Jesus in you! He has made you a new person!" That night, Jesus Christ forever changed my life! I had a new goal—serving Him with all my heart. I had a new purpose that is found in the Savior's powerful words, "*Seek the Kingdom of God above all else, and live righteously, and He will give you everything you need*" (Matthew 6:33, NLT). That night, Paul's words became my testimony, "*This means that anyone who belongs to Christ has become a new person. The old life is gone; a new life has begun*" (2 Corinthians 5:17, NLT)! Everyone, especially my precious parents, saw an amazing difference in me. I did a lot of asking for forgiveness where I had previously wronged people. Then, that fall when I attended high school, asking for forgiveness began again as I asked several fellow students and teachers to forgive me. I even began being seen with a new crowd. Truly, Jesus Christ can make anyone's life new. I know because if he can do it for me, he will do it for you! The Apostle Paul announced, "For I can do everything through Christ, who gives me strength" (Philippians 4:13, NLT). Through Jesus Christ, YOU CAN!

Dr. Adrian Rogers has said, "A faith that cannot be tried cannot be trusted." Oh, how true! God does try our faith. During my junior year at school, my faith was tried. Then, at a denominational youth gathering during our Christmas break, I roomed with a fellow high school student. We were friends, but not close friends. After that time, we became close friends. He shared a burden on his heart with me. As I encouraged him and prayed for him, he said, "Wayne, you ought to be a minister." I just laughed and said, "Oh, no. I don't think God wants me for that. I'll just teach English and coach basketball and baseball. I'll just share my faith in those circles." This was the first of many comments on that order. Then, camp came again. This time, God began to deal with me about ministry. In that time, I knew from a definite calling from Him that I was to be a minister of the gospel of Jesus Christ. So, I began seeking to walk in that road. I had a wonderful pastor at the First United Methodist Church in Coffeyville, Kansas, Dr. Robert Kendall. He was a blessing to guide me, even though some denominational officials tried to discourage me. Then, the big challenge came. Dr. Kendall was transferred to another pastorate.

Another minister, who did not share Dr. Kendall's views about ministry, my belief system, my calling, or me, became the pastor. In a very negative episode with my parents, he became my first serious challenge. I failed. In pain, disbelief, anger, and disappointment, I began my two-and-a-half-year rebellious journey away from the Lord. I dropped out of Coffeyville Community College and shifted from working part-time to working full-time at Bynum's Men's Wear. Jonah took one boat to his Nineveh. I took every boat that I could find. I had never had a minister hurt my family or me like this one. I thought I could not minister outside that system. Oh, how blind my limited faith was! Oh, how narrow was my view of God's call. That story, however, began to change. I worked for a wonderful man, J. D. Akard, at Bynum's Men's Wear in Coffeyville. His good friend, Dale Hawkins, and he asked to talk with me one afternoon. Mr. Hawkins suggested that I would be a good coach for their church's junior high boys' basketball team. Was I ever interested! Then, this line came from Mr. Hawkins, "Now, Wayne, you will have to attend church at least one Sunday each month." Did that ever challenge me since I had totally dropped out of church and was totally running from God! However, I did enjoy that age group and that sport. So, reluctantly, but determined, I agreed.

On my first visit to Coffeyville's First Baptist Church, I was so loved by the people and so blessed by Rev. Glenn Muncy and his message that I never stopped going. After attending a few Sundays, I made an appointment with Rev. Muncy and told him that I was a Christian, but I needed to be baptized. A week later, I was baptized on that Sunday evening. A couple of months later, I again met with our pastor and shared my ministry calling with him. He affirmed, encouraged me, and pledged to help me. A few weeks later, I stood one Sunday evening and preached a message to that congregation, who later licensed me to the gospel ministry. About four months later, a friend of mine, who was then pastoring the Central Baptist Church of rural Coffeyville, asked me to preach in his absence. He returned on the next Sunday, offered his resignation to become pastor of another congregation, and asked if I would consider preaching for them. Becoming their pulpit supply for a few Sundays led to being the congregation's interim pastor. After serving as interim pastor for the summer, the Central Baptist Church called me to be their pastor. On June 20, 1971, that church led in my ministerial ordination. One denomination's minister said, "YOU CAN'T." But, by the grace of God, two other denominations said, "YOU CAN!"

That was the beginning of God using Gail and me in several

pastoral situations. From the Central Baptist Church, the Lord led me to the following positions:

- Pastor, Friendship Southern Baptist Church, Parsons, Kansas;
- Senior Pastor, North Park Baptist Church in Moberly, Missouri;
- Pastor, First Baptist Church, Climax Springs, Missouri;
- Senior Pastor, Ely Baptist Church, Kennett, Missouri;
- Senior Pastor, First Baptist Church, Baxter Springs, Kansas;
- Senior Pastor, Parkview Southern Baptist Church, Wichita, Kansas;
- Senior Pastor, First Baptist Church, Junction City, Kansas;
- Senior Pastor, Lakeview Baptist Church, Battle Creek, Michigan, and
- Senior Pastor, First Baptist Church, Coffeyville, Kansas.

Three times, we were contacted by the Senior Pastor Search Committee of the Lakeview Baptist Church in Battle Creek, Michigan. At that point, God had placed us for over six years in Junction City, Kansas, where I was the senior pastor of the First Baptist Church. Mr. Charlie Kuepfer, who later became a very close friend, was the chairman of that committee from Battle Creek. In that third telephone call, he said, "Wayne, we feel so strongly that you are our person that we are willing to fly your family and you here for a few days to look at what we have, meet with some of us, and then decide what God would have you to do."

Well, the rest is history. We did go to that awesome congregation and serve with them. God was really working in our midst. The church was growing. We were on the radio every day with our program, "The Winner's Circle." Then, in the midst of

OF SUDDEN REALIZATION, INSPIRATION, AND INSIGHT FROM 26 PROFESSIONAL MEN

all the progress, which even included dialogue about television ministry, I began having problems with memory. In Junction City, I had suffered a cerebral hemorrhage that went totally undiagnosed. My new physician in Battle Creek did not notice it either. Then, Gail and our church secretary noticed that my memory was getting worse. I preached with notes and helps that I had not previously needed. The congregation did not realize a problem was beginning to mushroom. Gail confided in a nurse who was a member of our church. She recommended a physician in a nearby city. After three visits to this physician, I was referred to the University of Michigan Medical Center's Neurological Department for evaluation.

This group of doctors found that I had previously suffered from a cerebral hemorrhage and was suffering from Organic Amnesic Disorder. They told us that I would not be able to preach anymore nor could I stand before a congregation that I dearly loved and greatly appreciated, and I needed to express to them my regrets to offer the resignation that had to be made. The stress on my brain was of great concern at that time because doctors feared that mental pressure could cause more damage. The memory was worsening and kept me from remembering people's names, recognizing people that I should have known, or doing my daily routine at home as well as at work. Upon recommendation of the medical team, we returned to our home area of Kansas to be near our family. The medical team also recommended a neuropsychologist in Tulsa, Oklahoma, to be my specialist. His evaluation at that time was that I would never be in ministry again. In fact, he said that if I was able at all after recovery, I might be able to do custodial work. He was not too certain of my abilities to do even that.

Almost two years later, that same specialist said that I was a miracle. He explained that I was the most neurologically damaged individual that he had ever seen who had made such a recovery. This doctor said that I could begin slowly by doing pulpit supply work for two months. Then, I would be available for interim pastorates and ultimately pastoring. Again, the words of man said,

"YOU CAN'T!" But, by a miracle of God, I was told, "YOU CAN!"

After doing pulpit supply work in area churches, our home church, the First Baptist Church of Coffeyville, Kansas, needed a pastor. So, they first asked me to do pulpit supply work for a few months. Then, I was called as their interim senior pastor with the understanding that I would be a candidate for that position. For several months, I served in that position.

One Sunday morning, a Senior Pastor Search Committee from another church appeared in the sanctuary at First Baptist Church. After meeting with them, we agreed to consider their position and waited to hear from them. Were we in for a surprise! Upon our arrival at church that night, the chairman of the Senior Pastor Search Committee of the First Baptist Church in Coffeyville asked Gail and me to meet with their committee on that evening after the worship service. We met, listened to each of their hearts and their reasons for us as their choice. Then we told them that we first must talk with the chairman of the other search committee and discuss this matter with him. We were first committed to that committee. They agreed and were willing to wait. So, after talking on the next day with that congregation's search committee chairman, we were ethically released by them to pursue communication with the Coffeyville committee. The Lord led us to come to the First Baptist Church of Coffeyville. However, before making that announcement to the Coffeyville committee, we followed ethics and made that announcement to the other church's committee. After almost ten years as senior pastor of the First Baptist Church of Coffeyville, I felt God's leadership to resign because I was facing several health issues that needed attention.

Seven major illnesses had all arrived simultaneously upon my body. My weight had dropped from being overweight at 248 pounds to 164 pounds.

Five trips to the Mayo Clinic and several doctors later, God has worked an amazing work of healing. Although I still deal with fibromyalgia and back issues, the remaining issues have all gone.

God, in the meantime, was working to restore my body and renew my mind so that I would be able to minister through the ministry that He led me to found and to direct, Hope for Your Day Ministries, Inc.

Hope for Your Day Ministries, Inc. is an online ministry that publishes blogs on several sites: LinkedIn, Twitter (@hopeforyourday), Facebook (hopeforyourday), and a website, www.hopeforyourday.com. Beginning in the very near future, that site will also host our podcasts, which will have daily devotionals, Sunday messages, and other items to be added later. This ministry includes my availability as a speaker for seminars on various subjects (evangelism, church growth, leadership, humor, grief, pastoral care, and revivals.). Also, I have been blessed by local pulpit supply ministry.

My first book is now in the final stages of publication. The Lord has given me three other books that I shall give to him for publication in the days ahead. Now I am no longer on disability and, by the grace of God, am back into ministry in my retirement years. When I first became ill, doctors doubted that I would ever minister again. Some even said I would not. But, when man says no, God has the final word! Yes, you knew I was going to say it. The words of man again said, "YOU CAN'T!" But, God said, "YOU CAN!"

The Lord has blessed Gail and me through another time of trial as well. At the age of two, our son, Aaron, became very feverish and was not well all day. Even though the doctor was in his office on the other side of Wichita, Kansas, Gail made an appointment for Aaron. The doctor only found a sore throat and prescribed Tylenol to control the fever. On the way out, the nurse said, "I know you are an overprotective mother, but you don't have to bring him in every time he is running a temperature." Gail knew her child was sick and didn't listen to that comment. That Wednesday evening, Gail stayed home with our son. As I was delivering the Wednesday evening message at Parkview Southern Baptist Church in Wichita,

Kansas, one of our men came running from the kitchen after serving our Wednesday evening meal. He came running toward me, stopped, and whispered in my ear that Gail was on her way to the hospital with Aaron and that I needed to meet them in front of the church. Aaron was convulsing when they met me. We arrived at Wesley Medical Center where he was admitted from the emergency room to the pediatric intensive care unit.

  That next morning, the doctor told me that he was suffering from spinal meningitis. When I asked if she thought that he would live, tears came into her eyes (she had a girl the same age.). She replied that they did not expect him to live. I went to the chapel and prayed. I simply gave myself and our son to the Lord. I called each former pastorate and requested prayer. I called a person from our church and Gail called family. On Father's Day, fourteen days later, God allowed us to bring him home from the hospital. What a miracle! We were told, "YOU CAN'T!" But God intervened in this case to glorify his name and said, "YOU CAN!"

  On December 6, 2012, we received another phone call. This was truly the most difficult trial of faith that both of us have ever experienced. Our daughter-in-law called on that afternoon. Aaron had been wounded in a gun accident. After assuring her that our love and prayers were with her and that we were on our way to the hospital, I immediately called Gail and Sara, our daughter. All of us rushed to the Mercy Hospital emergency room in Independence, Kansas. Aaron was unconscious from the time of the wound and was lying on that emergency room bed, unresponsive. Next, he was transported by helicopter to Via Christi Medical Center in Wichita, Kansas. He suffered a wound through the lower hemispheres of his brain. Again, prayer was offered. His wife and her family and we and our family prayed, waited, and hoped. No, a miracle did not happen this time. Our twenty-seven-year-old son moved out of his body and into the presence of our Lord.

  That afternoon, a flashback came to me as we saw his death. I remembered a five-year-old boy crawling into my lap and asking,

"Daddy, how can I have Jesus in my heart?" I realized that he did not know what he was doing even at the age of five and led him to Jesus that night.

Then, we talked about baptism. That was on Monday evening, and no more was discussed about baptism. On Friday evening, he again came into my lap before the evening meal. He said, "Daddy, I got Jesus in my heart. You said when Jesus is in your heart you need to be baptized. So, when are you going to let me be baptized?" I smiled and said, "Son, when do you want to be baptized?" He wanted Gail's mother present. So, we called Gail's parents, Aaron told them what had happened and asked them to come for his baptism. They did, and he was baptized. But, before I put him under the water, he looked at Grandma Elsheimer and smiled his biggest smile. He really loved his grandmother!

You say, "Wayne, God did not answer your prayer." Oh, no. God perfectly healed Aaron because God brought him into the presence of Jesus, who welcomed him home—and Grandma Elsheimer was probably next in line after Jesus! We may have been told, "YOU CAN'T!" But, hear me, dear friends, even in death, YOU CAN through Jesus Christ! Jesus announced, "...*I am the resurrection and the life. Anyone who believes in Me will live, even after dying. Everyone who lives in Me and believes in Me will never ever die...*" (John 11:25–26, NLT). The apostle Paul reminds us that when we move out of our earthly bodies, we move immediately into the presence of our Lord Jesus Christ (2 Corinthians 5:8).

For forty-four years, Gail and I have been blessed in that marriage that began on January 8, 1971, at the First Baptist Church in Coffeyville, Kansas. God has blessed my life in so many ways and in wonderful days because Gail has been by my side. In every time of trial, she has been with me and has been a blessing for me. The road before us has had a lot of unexpected twists and turns. We have been blessed with two wonderful children, Sara and Aaron. Sara, her husband, and their three children are very active in their church. Also, God has blessed us with a lot of beautiful people in every church that we have pastored and in every community where we have lived. God gave us great people to help us with a formal education and directed that education into a life and ministry that has gone places that we never dreamed of going. Gail's career as an educator and mine as a minister, plus ours as a team in ministry together, has taught us many things. The lesson that God has taught me repeatedly, and only a few instances have been shared in this chapter, is that resilience is the key to a winning life with Jesus Christ.

A bump in the road or a stump in the path is not a signal to stop, but an invitation to seek God's help and to keep on going and growing. God loves us and will never lead us where He cannot get the glory from our life. Every step we take with God is one step in a journey that takes us from where we are to where we can be with Him. Someone has told you that "YOU CAN'T"? Remember what Jesus taught us: "*...But with God everything is possible*" (Matthew 19:26b, NLT). Hear this—hear this loud and clear—"YOU CAN!" When a dream dies, don't die with it. Find that new dream with the Lord, and he will show you that with his help, "YOU CAN!" Every broken dream is a new opportunity to look to God for His dream and dream again with Him! Someone wisely said, "If one dream should fall apart and break into a thousand pieces, never be afraid to pick up one of those pieces and begin again!"

Bio of Dr. Charles Wayne Norton

Dr. Charles Wayne Norton was born on July 3, 1948, in Cherryvale, Kansas. His parents were Charles H. and Pearl M. (Sims) Norton. He is a graduate of Labette County High School in Altamont, Kansas (1966); Coffeyville Community College, Coffeyville, Kansas (AA, 1971); Southwest Baptist University, Bolivar, Missouri (BA in Religion/Psychology, 1977), and Luther Rice Seminary, Lithonia, Georgia (MA in Ministry, 1991; M. Div., 1985; D. Min, 1988). He also attended Hannibal-LaGrange College in Hannibal, Missouri, Southwestern Baptist Theological Seminary in Fort Worth, Texas, and Luther Rice Seminary in Lithonia, Georgia (in the master's in psychology program).

Dr. Norton has served as the pastor of Central Baptist Church in Coffeyville, Kansas; Friendship Southern Baptist Church in Parsons, Kansas; and First Baptist Church in Climax Springs, Missouri. He has served as the senior pastor of North Park Baptist Church in Moberly, Missouri; Ely Baptist Church in Kennett, Missouri; First Baptist Church in Baxter Springs, Kansas; Parkview

Southern Baptist Church in Wichita, Kansas; First Baptist Church in Junction City, Kansas; Lakeview Baptist Church in Battle Creek, Michigan, and First Baptist Church in Coffeyville, Kansas.

Having served in several denominational leadership positions, Dr. Norton has also served as the president of local ministerial alliances in three cities. He has been very active in local organizations and ministries in each city where he has served. Along with this, he has been a speaker for radio, television, and revivals as well as a writer of pastor's columns for local newspapers. Currently, Dr. Norton serves as the founder and executive director of Hope for Your Day Ministries, Inc. This ministry seeks to share Jesus Christ as God's only person, plan, and possibility of salvation for everyone. His first book is currently in the final stages of editing. On Mondays through Fridays, Dr. Norton's blogs appear on LinkedIn, Twitter (@hopeforyourday), Facebook (hopeforyourday), and the ministry's web page (www.hopeforyourday.com). In the very near future, the web page will become a site for podcasting messages, devotional thoughts, and teachings by Dr. Norton.

Dr. Norton married Gail Elsheimer on January 8, 1971, at the First Baptist Church in Coffeyville, Kansas. Dr. and Mrs. Norton are the parents of two children, Sara and Aaron (Aaron died in 2012), and have three grandchildren. Currently, Dr. and Mrs. Norton are living in southeastern Kansas. They minister and serve in their retirement years as God gives them the opportunity through Hope for Your Day Ministries, Inc. Jesus Christ is the "HOPE FOR YOUR DAY!"

A-ha Moments
Sean Evers, PhD

The box truck was parked under the trees on the unpaved driveway next to my uncle's house. Each morning, my father would leave to service his route before I left for school. He would get home around 4:00 and then we would spend about an hour reloading the truck from the warehouse that was our basement. About once a week, a tractor would come to unload new product to replenish the stock. On those days, deliveries would start later. Working on commission was a strong motivator for the sole provider of a growing family.

We had one of those 1950s homes on a small lot where the garage was under the house and the driveway was a steep incline. Backing the truck or the trailer into the narrow space was an art. Many of the tractor drivers refused to back down the driveway, so my father would take over and back their truck down for them to make unloading easier.

My father had been a sickly child. He had rheumatic fever that resulted in his having a heart condition for life. He also had a vision problem that was never fully explained to me, but that necessitated serious eye surgery when he was a child. The only story he would tell about the eye surgery was that the surgeon was so unsure of the success of the procedure that they bandaged a religious medal of Saint Teresa in with the postoperative bandages in hopes that she would intercede in his healing. The surgery saved his sight, but he had what he described as triple vision in one eye for the rest of his life, a fact he didn't share with me until he retired. A statue of

Saint Teresa was the first significant addition to the garden in front of our house after we moved in. It stood there on a stone pedestal for decades.

When my father quit high school in his senior year to join the Army, he should have been rated 4-F because of his heart and vision. He talked his way into the Army, failing the eye test since he could not see the big E on the chart without his glasses. The story was that the doctor told him to walk forward until he could see the letters on the chart, and he walked up to the wall, traced the big E with his nose, and then laughed. He ended up a combat medic landing in Europe as part of the D-Day invasion.

My father was the social one of the family. He was a joiner. He joined the Boy Scouts to be a leader as I approached the scouting age. He later joined the Knights of Columbus, an interest that he kept for the remainder of his life, moving through the various offices both local and statewide. Inevitable with his involvement in these groups was the fact that he worked hard at the tasks he was given and succeeded. Along the way he involved me in rehabilitating the abandoned building the organization bought, learned to manage a club bar after the prior volunteer manager ran it into debt, learned accounting to manage the accounts of the club, reopened the club pool and snack bar, and got me my first jobs as badge checker, short order cook, and finally lifeguard.

Throughout his work, social involvements, and other interests, one theme always stood out. In whatever interest he had, he always worked hard to see it succeed. He also always ended up as the one person everyone seemed to seek out to discuss things with. Whether it was his older brother, my uncle Vic, or the many members of scouting or the members of the club, they all seemed to seek out his counsel when it came to difficult decisions. Although he didn't graduate high school until he received his GED in his 60s, he had a wealth of common sense that was recognized by those who knew him.

My uncle Vic always lived close by. When I was a child,

he lived with my grandparents in the apartment behind my grandfather's store and we lived upstairs over the store. When I was age 10, we moved to our own home near the Jersey shore in one of those rapidly growing, lower middle-class communities where houses—like rabbits—seemed to multiply overnight. My uncle Brother (that's what everyone called him, since indeed he was my father's brother) had moved there several years before and was enjoying the benefits of the more suburban lifestyle. Within a year of our move, Uncle Vic bought the empty lot next to our house and began building his own home, one he would eventually share with his parents until their death. Once again, he was close by, and since he never had a regular job, he was always available.

Uncle Vic emigrated from Italy as a boy of about 7. My grandfather had emigrated a year earlier than the rest of the family to get a job and set up the household. Uncle Vic was placed in public school. He did not know one word of English. He once talked about the teacher who discovered that he couldn't understand what was going on in class, about a year after he was enrolled, and helped him learn English, but he never mentioned it again. He also never seemed resentful that no one noticed. Uncle Vic left formal school in eighth grade (whether he finished elementary school or not is part of family history that is now lost). He was always good with his hands. He apprenticed and became a machinist. This line of work matched his meticulous work ethic and appealed to his fascination about how things worked. One day, I asked him about school and he pointed to the Encyclopedia Americana that he kept prominently in his house in the bookcase by the front door. He said without any hint of pride, "I knew I didn't know anything, so I saved up and bought the set one book at a time." This was a popular way to afford an encyclopedia at the time. "I read each volume from cover to cover before I bought the next one," he added. It never came up again, although I still am amazed at the breadth and depth of his knowledge and understanding of the world.

Uncle Vic worked as a machinist in Arizona for the

government during WWII. After the war, when my grandfather lost his leg to an uninsured New York City cab, he came back to New Jersey to take care of him and my grandmother until they died. He never worked as a machinist again, but rather in my grandfather's tailor shop. He had saved the money he made during the war and, together with some funds my grandfather had saved, invested successfully in the stock market. Those investments served as his nest egg for the rest of his life. He lived modestly yet comfortably, and he never had a credit card or a bank loan.

If it could be made out of wood or metal, he could make it in his basement shop. He would be insulted if anyone offered him money for a project or repair. He enjoyed the work and the challenge. His house was highlighted by his wood carvings, handmade chess set, oil paintings, and other projects that interested him. Often they were the result of having a piece of scrap wood that called out to him to become something. It was always an adventure to have some school project or problem that needed to be solved and turn to him to help out. In a calm way that only he could manifest, he would think about it and then one day the task would be done, whether that meant he spent the time to teach me how to do it or just worked on the project himself, seemingly fascinated by the new challenge.

Uncle Vic and my father worked together on large projects, like building Uncle Vic's house or adding a room to our small home next door. They were an interesting pair. My father was aggressive and not detail oriented. He would push ahead somehow knowing that whatever project they tackled they would figure it out and sometimes make it work with a little extra whack from the hammer. Uncle Vic would sit back and analyze the problem and eventually be pushed into the solution by my father's impatience. Over the years, they built two houses together from the ground up. I remember my father drawing the blueprints and he and Vic arguing over this detail or that, but both resorting to some second-hand reference book to figure out the details. I think they did hire an electrician to wire the

OF SUDDEN REALIZATION, INSPIRATION, AND INSIGHT FROM 26 PROFESSIONAL MEN

panel box in order to pass inspection, but the rest they worked out together.

Uncle Brother was a very different story. He was an artist, a cartoonist by trade. I never knew him to do anything else. He was in the Coast Guard working as a cartoonist during WWII. After the war, he continued in his profession, working as one of the early artists for Marvel Comics before setting out on his own and becoming a political and sports cartoonist. He worked for several different newspapers, ending his career with a multi-decade run as the political cartoonist for the New York News, which at that time was the newspaper with the largest circulation in the world. It was the perfect place for a political cartoonist who wanted to have his voice and opinion heard.

He lived with my aunt and cousins about two miles away in a modest home in a section of town that was a resort community. During the winter, the area was very quiet with many of the houses empty until summer, when the entire area was teaming with families enjoying their summer vacation. During the summer, there was always something going on at my uncle's house: a barbecue, a sail on his small sailboat, or just a visit to hang out. He worked out of a studio my father and Uncle Vic built for him in his detached garage.

His studio always looked like a tornado had just happened. His drawing board was always clear. Next to it was a chaos of pens, paints, brushes and charcoal. The floor was several feet deep with old drawings, rejected ideas, and originals all mixed together. He had a filing system that only he could understand. In the corner of the studio hung a white leather heavy bag that he used to work out with when he couldn't get to his usual gym, where he worked out with various boxers, some of whom ended up being famous professionals.

In his unpaved driveway in front of the studio, he would often set up a ping pong table, a popular family pastime. "I can beat you using the sole of my shoe," he once challenged me in ping pong.

A confident adolescent, I knew that he must be wrong. No one could beat me in ping pong with a shoe. I was wrong.

You never knew what was going to happen at my uncle's house. Sometimes he would talk about something interesting that happened at work, like the day the president called to complain about a cartoon, a trip he took with the USO to visit wounded soldiers in Southeast Asia, or the night he entertained the treasurer of the state of Nevada, who was a high school friend. The few I recall were fascinating to an adolescent, and seemed to come up by accident. Looking back, I know there were many other interesting stories and experiences that were never discussed. They were presented in an off-handed way with the same interest as might be shown in a Little League game, helping with a school project, or attending a high-school show.

I graduated from high school, and there was no question that I was to graduate from college. No member of my family had ever graduated from college before. There was pressure to major in something concrete and practical. The cost of college was a strain on my family. College began with the goal of becoming a physician. Growing up, I had no professional role models other than the family doctor. I once accompanied my parents to a lawyer's office and was overly awed by all the books. I could never become a lawyer. After two years of pre-med/biochemistry, something was wrong. My skills, interests, and talents didn't flourish in the lab. After much consternation, I changed my major to English with a focus on creative writing. I graduated in a field of study not really understood by my family, and not very practical if you want to make a living.

In my senior year, I took a psychology course in order to offer a fresh perspective on the characters in *Paradise Lost*. Little did I know that it would lead me in a totally different career direction. Psychology, especially as a profession, made less sense to my family than an undergraduate degree in English. I had become a high-school teacher after college. I had chosen a practical job that my family understood and that offered security, but my interest in psychology grew more than my interest in teaching. Pursuing a graduate degree in psychology with an undergraduate degree in English was a challenge. That initial challenge was compounded when I decided to continue my education to receive a doctoral degree in clinical psychology. Leaving the security of being a tenured high-school teacher to work as a marginally paid psychology intern brought many questions and quizzical looks at family gatherings.

More than a decade after receiving my undergraduate degree, I earned my doctorate and went directly into private practice. Years after being in a traditional clinical practice, those physiology and biochemistry courses that didn't work out as an undergraduate seemed interesting again and led me to become one of the first psychologists to receive a post-doctoral master's in clinical psychopharmacology. Somehow I had come full circle.

The three men that influenced my adolescence gave me the belief that anything was possible if you dedicated your effort to it, did the work, and didn't take no for an answer. Each man offered a different set of traits to model. The hard work of loading, unloading, and driving a delivery truck, the smell of fresh cut wood, a hint of sawdust in the air, the fading twang of the electric saw blade, the ability to have an independent opinion that was heard around the country each day, and being beaten in ping pong by someone who used his shoe as a paddle make up the strongest memories of adolescence. They form the experiences that shaped my adolescence. Three different men each offered me a different view of how to be a man. Each one was personally different, with different interests and different personal values, but each one was available to the tall, skinny, bookish adolescent that didn't seem to fit anyone's idea of what adolescence should be.

Each of the men that shaped my childhood and teenage years offered something different. Hard work and family were the common threads that tied each of them together, but in almost every other way I can think of, they were different. My dad was a hard-working man who overcame his physical limitations to have a full and active life. My Uncle Vic didn't have a family of his own, so he adopted ours. He was a best friend to both me and my father. His calm, methodical approach to any problem made everything seem possible. If it could be built, it was buildable; if it could be learned and it was in a book, it could be learned. And finally my Uncle Brother showed me that it is possible, no matter where you came from, through your skill and talent, to have an impact on the world.

Three men, none of whom graduated from college, one who just completed elementary school, one who received his GED in his 60s, and one who left college to join the service. None of them understood my career choice and the path I took to get there, but all of them were supportive and each one contributed to the mosaic of what it is to be successful.

Bio of Dr. Sean R. Evers

Dr. Sean R. Evers is a clinical psychologist in private practice in Manasquan, New Jersey. He has been in private practice for over 30 years in the same area. He completed his undergraduate degree in English at Marietta College. He received his first master's degree from the New School for Social Research in Psychology and his doctorate in clinical psychology from the Florida Institute of Technology, School of Professional Psychology. After being in practice for 20 years, he returned to school, receiving his second master's degree in a new field for psychologists, clinical psychopharmacology, from Fairleigh Dickinson University.

Dr. Evers was president of the New Jersey Psychological Association in 2013 and of the New Jersey Psychological Foundation in 2014. He is a founding director of the New Jersey Academy of Medical Psychologists and the Center for Posttraumatic Studies.

Dr. Evers began treating traumatized war veterans in the early 1980s and continues to work in that specialty as part of his clinical practice. This interest led to his becoming a presenter at veterans' conferences throughout the country. His interest in clinical psychopharmacology for psychologists resulted in his receiving the award for Outstanding Contribution to the Advancement of Pharmacotherapy at the National Level at the American Psychological Association National Convention in 2013.

Once a Dork, Always a Dork
Joseph Singleton

I have always been attracted to the opposite sex. When I was young, I would always play with the girls in my class versus the other boys. We played games like dress up, family, My Little Pony, and of course (my favorite when the parents were not around), doctor. I did play with the guys every once in awhile, but it just seemed that my first choice was the girls. I mean, I played tag, basketball, baseball, football, and the other things young men did at that age. The only problem was, I came to find out when puberty hit, was that I was shy when it came to courtship; I had no issues talking to women as long as I was not trying to be their boyfriend. The nerd in me (I'll explain later) is what allowed me to talk to women, but the player in me was a dork and could not "close any deals." "I was never issued a players card," from a saying we used back in the day. For those who do not know the difference, here are the definitions:

A nerd is someone who has an excessive concern for their academic performance.

A dork is someone who is socially inept.

A geek is someone who has an abnormally intense interest in a particular subject.

My parents knew that I really enjoyed playing sports, especially the sport my mom taught me how to play: basketball. Like many kids, I wanted to be a professional athlete. Well, my parents, like most, were full of wisdom and life experiences. They told me of many athletes they knew of that did not make it to become a professional athlete and the possibility of getting hurt in the first year and not being able to support myself because I did not focus on my grades as a backup plan. Like many other kids, it did not really sink in until I saw a Hollywood movie dramatizing a failed athlete.

I have always been fascinated with airplanes, which made me a geek at times, but these life lessons turned me into a nerd. The only difference was that I was not that excessive about my academic performance, as it came rather easy to me. (I mean, how hard is it to listen and regurgitate what was said in class on a test or quiz?) This is what made the girls come to me for help. And yes, I was attracted to a few of them, but the dorky player in me could not talk to them. It also did not help that my parents did not buy me clothes that fit—loosely or in style—and not from K-Mart. I did not complain though, because my parents were able to provide for me better than their parents were able to provide for them. But to sum up, I dressed like a dork, and my inner player was a dork, so I was labeled a dork, which drove me to become a dork. However, the difference between me and the typical dork was that I was actually pretty decent at playing sports, so I coined the term "smart jock."

Because of my skill level, I was able to be the schools' chameleon, meaning I could hang out with the nerds, dorks, and geeks as well as the "popular" kids, like the athletes and cheerleaders; I just did not talk much when I did, in fear of saying the wrong thing.

When hanging out with the unpopular-labeled individuals, I could tune in to my "geek-ness." I even started drawing airplanes, mostly fighters. I have always liked airplanes: probably because my father was in the Air Force, and from Top Gun. It wasn't because of the story, or the actors that played in it, although the soundtrack was pretty good, but it was because of the F-14 Tomcat, my second-favorite plane (the first is the F/A-18 Hornet). Most of my drawings were a mixture of two, or anything I could build out of my Lego pieces and other building toys from the day.

When hanging out with the popular-labeled individuals, I could talk sports when needed because I would actually watch professional sports on television at that time. I mean, how else was I supposed to learn how to get better? I would break down the movements like they were the teacher and I was the student in class. I would rehearse the movements in my mind until I was able to do them in person, as if the movement was homework. After perfecting the moves, I would use them against my friends, as if it was a graded test, and make minor adjustments as needed (did I mention I was a nerd at times?).

Unfortunately, I started to realize that a lot of the professionals were in it only for the money. The realization hit during the 90s when just about all the major professional sport leagues went on strike trying to get more money—more money to play a game, a game that most kids and young adults play for fun. These strikes, made me realize that the game the professionals played was not a game, it was a job, and why would I want to watch someone else work? This realization disgusted me and to this day, I cannot watch an entire game of any professional sport except the Super Bowl because of the funny commercials. After this realization, and remembering the lessons my omniscient parents taught me growing up, I made another realization: I have to change my plans and work for a living.

As I was growing up, my father would always remind me about when it was going to be "my turn" in life. It took me a while to finally understand what he meant, but when I realized it, it was almost like a deafening blow to the senses: I realized that I could not just come home and play sports or ask for money whenever I or my friends wanted to go somewhere for the rest of my life. I mean, I had the typical under-the-table jobs that adolescent boys did at that age, like cutting the neighbors' yards, pulling weeds, and other manual, labor-intensive employment for the weekends. But the moment that it hit me was when one of my friends got us a job doing yard work for an elderly man. It would be my first paycheck.

I remember the day like it was yesterday. It was a sunny, summer day with a hint of pine in the breeze (we were living in Washington State at the time) that felt like a warm bath on the skin. I held out my hand after working for ten hours to receive a $45 check. In my mind, the day grew cloudy and thunderstorms were on the horizon as soon as I saw the number 45. The man began to explain, almost instinctively: "$5 per hour, right, and I believe you two took a 30-minute lunch and a few breaks." I looked around his complex and just started thinking, "you cheap bastard." The guy had a DeLorean, a car similar to the one in *Back to the Future*, in mint condition, a four-car garage, and a huge house sitting on at least three acres of land, and you could not give us an extra $5 each? I looked at my friend and he seemed to be as happy as a child who had just received an ice cream cone on that hot day. What made it worse, when I confronted him about the smile and pleasantries he expressed, he told me it was a lot of money and could not wait to go back the next weekend. As we sat on the city bus headed back home, I started thinking about why he would say what he said. To him, $45 may be a lot of money, since he had six siblings and I am sure they had to "stretch the dollar." So I started planning my life because I was not going to have a job where I had to do that much work and get paid that little. So, as we returned weekly to work for the "cheap bastard," I concentrated on what I wanted to do in life and had it laid out before I was a freshman in high school.

I decided that sports would no longer be my profession, so I went back to what I enjoyed most: airplanes. I researched what jobs revolved around this particular form of mass transportation and decided that I was going to be an aeronautical engineer

OF SUDDEN REALIZATION, INSPIRATION, AND INSIGHT FROM 26 PROFESSIONAL MEN

so that I could be an aircraft designer—I mean, I already had conceptual designs from when I was in elementary school. I would go to college and get married by the time I was 25 years old and have two kids, one boy and one girl, in that order, before I was 30 years old. And I was going to design something so great that I could tell my kids, grandkids, and future kids who will not stay off my lawn that I designed that plane, or that piece of a plane, as it flew by. The only thing remained was deciding which college to go to.

After a short time, before the Christmas break of my freshman year in high school, I chose to go to the University of Washington, since it was not too far from where my parents were living and I could ease into this thing called "adulthood." Unfortunately, I started to hate school even more than usual. Having to get up at 6 a.m. to catch the bus at 7 a.m. and be in class before 7:30 a.m. was too much, especially since I had to stay up late doing homework after working or playing a late basketball game (I played on the school team).

When I reached the appropriate age to work and be paid "over-the-table" as a W2 employee, I got a job washing dishes at a fancy restaurant in Olympia, Washington. It was fun at the start, but after the "honeymoon" phase was over (two hours after my first day), I realized that I had taken a step in the wrong direction, and this job quickly became a "means to the end." It took awhile, but I found another job and quit the restaurant business. One of my basketball teammates, who also worked there and had helped me get the job, told me that they said I was fired, but I did quit, just not in a professional manner.

I actually liked my next job working at ShopKo in Lacey. I enjoyed working with the customers and working in the store, until the day minimum wage was raised. I started the job at $5.25 an hour. After a year of working there, I had received an "excellent" rating on my annual review, after being nominated to be "employee of the month" twice, and winning once, and

I received a $0.23 raise in my hourly pay, coincidentally to be effective the same day as the $0.25 per hour rise in the minimum wage was to be effective.

So again, remembering it like it was yesterday: it was a sunny, summer day with a hint of pine in the breeze as I walked to the payroll window after clocking in to start my shift on the payday that occurred after my pay increase and raise in minimum wage. I held out my hand to receive my check from payroll, knowing that my check was going to be a big one since I was going see $5.73, a $0.48 per wage increase, next to the number of hours I worked those past two weeks. I tore open the envelope and read $5.50 per hour as my wage.

To this day, I swear I heard it thundering outside. I immediately ran to the nearest manager and started protesting. The response was obviously planned: "After your $0.23 raise, you were below the new minimum wage, so your wage had to be increased again to meet minimum wage." Then I asked about the new folks, and she confirmed that they were being paid the same amount. To say the least, it took a little while before I was able to go out on the floor.

That night, another realization occurred to me: I would not be able to support myself in college by only earning that amount of money. That conclusion resulted from my ignorance of the fact that there were student loans, which had been created for such instances. As I previously mentioned, I was pretty tired of being in school and, as we said in economics, I had reached "the point of diminishing returns" I was working hard to go to school, but feeling tired and not motivated throughout the process. I was stricken by the laziness bug.

The laziness that had consumed me was so great that I didn't even do the paperwork to apply to college or the Reserve Officers' Training Corps, commonly known as ROTC. The worst part was, for the University of Washington, all I had to do was apply and I would have been accepted according to the metrics chart that showed the possible acceptance ratings based on the applicant's grade point average and Scholastic Aptitude Test (SAT) or American College Testing (ACT) scores.

My grade point average was high enough, even though my SAT and ACT scores were just average, since I was—and still am—a dismal test taker when the test is timed. The only problem was that I did not know how I was going to pay, since I had not done any financial research due to my ignorance on the subject. I hadn't even started to ask the right questions. As for the ROTC application, all I had to do was fill out a bubble sheet and submit it. Moreover, out of all the countless A's I received during my tenure as a student, I actually received an F in economics, not because it was too hard, but because I was too lazy to do the work. I could have actually gotten a D if I had completed the last assignment, a report of some kind that would not have been too difficult had I read the textbook. At this point in life, I was acting like water—following the flow and taking the path of least resistance—and the extra amount of thinking I had to do for the economics class was too much of a mountain to climb. Let's just say that my high school should not have let me see my files because after reviewing them, I quickly realized that I did not need the class to graduate on time, since I had more than enough credits and a pretty high grade point average. I was tied with the 18th graduate from my high school as far as grade point average was concerned, but ranked at 22 since my last name started with an S. (At least, that's my story and I am sticking to it.) However, in reality, the number of significant figures probably went past the two decimal places shown on the report, which would numerically put me at 22.

Shortly after my 18th birthday in February 1997, my father, in his settled ways, asked me about my college applications and my plans after I graduated. After telling him that I had not applied to college and did not know what I was going to do, his response was, "I expect rent to be paid on the first of July since you graduate in June." To this day, I do not know if the word actually escaped my mouth, but I do know my facial expression was contorted to say "WHAT?!?!" and I do know that I said I would think of something to reassure him that before the end of summer, I was not going to be living there.

To this day, I do not quite remember what inspired me, but a few weeks later, I had enlisted into the Air Force as a delayed enlistee—signing the contract made me a third-generation Air Force enlistee. I do know that I remember seeing a commercial about the Montgomery GI Bill, but I think it was an Army commercial. The weeks leading up to signing the enlistment contract were actually quite interesting for me. My high school had sponsored a career day and all the military recruiters attended, and the Navy was the only service that brought an officer to their booth. It was weird; I do not know if it was a part of their training, but they seemed to know that I was a prime candidate.

The first booth I stopped at was the Navy/Marine booth, not because I wanted to join the Navy, but because my friends wanted to stop there (as I said before, I was water—just going with the flow). At some point in the conversation, our grades came up and I told them my average and almost immediately all the attention shifted to me. This did not surprise me, since they always want the best and brightest, and in my group, I was the best candidate grade-wise, which I'll explain later. When asked, I told them that I would like to be an aeronautical engineer. (At this point in time, I had just presented my capstone project on how to become an aeronautical engineer and what they did.) I also told them that I would love to be a pilot and fly, as I was thinking about the Top Gun movie. The recruiter's response indicated that Air Force pilots were second to those in the Navy, since naval aviators had to land on a moving target. My rebuttal was, "Yeah, that's probably true, but Air Force pilots don't have to live on a big boat for months on end. I don't like being confined." I did not tell him that I have been on aircraft carriers and had seen the amount of personal space that was available for each of its members on the boat—practically none, unless you were the captain of the ship. The Marine at the booth tried to persuade me to sign up with his branch, but outside of noticing that he wore the best-looking uniform in comparison to the others, I had no interest, due to the ignorance of not knowing what they did.

The next booth was for the Army. The conversation mirrored the conversation at the Navy/Marine booth and, once again, I was the center of attention. Even though I was "lost" and did not really know what I wanted to do after graduation, I was 100% sure that I was not going to join the Army. I grew up as an Air Force brat. I heard the stories from my father's peers and my family members. One particular story was told to me by my uncle. He was in the Army during Vietnam and my grandpa was in the Air Force during the same conflict.

One day, the enemy overran my uncle's unit and he escaped and ran into my grandfather's unit. After the challenge and response was completed and the perimeter guards eliminated the pursuers, my uncle found my grandpa (his stepfather). Cutting the story short, my uncle was surprised that the Air Force unit had warm water for a shower and clean white sheets to sleep in while in the field. Another story came to mind; it was told to me while I was visiting my father's office. One of his subordinates, who had been deployed during what is now referred to as the First Gulf War in the early 1990s in Iraq, asked me how to tell the difference between an Air Force tent and an Army tent. The answer was that the Air Force tents had an air conditioning unit hooked up to it.

I am not trying, nor will ever tell someone, to not join the Army, because I am not. What I am trying to say is that I have a particular lifestyle I have grown accustomed to—even on camping trips, we camp in a recreational vehicle, never in a tent, with a television set and microwave. The Army does not support this lifestyle, and I am extremely thankful that there are people in the world that can live that lifestyle and do the things that Army folks do, even when in war. For the "cost of freedom is not free."

The last military booth was the Air Force's booth. Again, the conversation was a "déjà vu" moment. However, this particular sell was easier for my group, nobody was singled out, and we all decided to go with the Air Force.

As I mentioned, within the group I was with for career day, I had the best grade point average. I am not saying they were not smart, because they were. I had book sense, while they had street sense and more common sense. In fact, while playing ball at the house of the same boy who thought $45 was a lot of money, one weekend during our eighth-grade year, his mom asked about grades. He told her what to expect on his report card; she gave a nonchalant nod, and looked at me. I told her, "I think I got an A-minus" (I was lazy, but smart). She asked, "What else?" My response was, "The A-minus will be my lowest grade." Her facial expression was a scolding look toward my friend; he defended himself, saying, "Yeah, ask him how well he does playing scrabble or thinking for himself." I hate to admit it, but he knew this was my weakness, and I admired him for it because we were so competitive that we studied our opponents to learn how to defeat them. I usually won when it came to playing sports, and he usually won when it came to playing card and board games.

Card and board games were where you had to think and predict probabilities, while sports were all about anticipating movements by watching your opponents' hips and gestures. In fact, half of my friends were this way. This just happened to be the makeup of the group I was in during career day.

A week after career day, we went to see the Air Force recruiters to make it official. The friend that worked with me

OF SUDDEN REALIZATION, INSPIRATION, AND INSIGHT FROM 26 PROFESSIONAL MEN

at the "cheap bastard's" house was not able to make it because his parents could not find his birth certificate—it turned out he was adopted overseas. (At least, I think that was the story.) My other friend told the recruiter that he wanted to someday be an FBI/CIA agent and thought that he would get a start on that path by being a member of the security forces (the Air Force's version of the Army's military police or a civilian cop). As I was just following the flow, I told him I wanted to do the same. The recruiter then explained that we needed to take the pre-Armed Services Vocational Aptitude Battery (ASVAB) test to see where we stood in relation to that career field.

After reviewing our results, my friend was told that he had to come back in take it again as he missed too many for that particular career field. He turned to me and asked if I really wanted to be part of the security forces, because my score suggested that I could choose any Air Force career path and security forces was the least desirable because of the possibility of having to guard a B-52 bomber on alert in North Dakota in the winter. I was with my father when he was stationed at Minot AFB, North Dakota, and to say the least, this lifestyle would fall under the "nondesirable" category.

When I got home that night, my father was pleased to hear that I had enlisted in the Air Force and reminded me that I needed to go to college and perhaps become an officer. This would not come up again until a particular day when I reported for my shift and was told about a situation where my shop chief, or manager, had scolded one of my peers for taking a second job to help support his growing family and not filling out the proper forms. This verbal assault was one of many that drove the shop members to dislike him.

At this point in time, I knew I had to be the voice of change, not with him in the shop on this day, but as an officer to set an example and be there for others who could wind up in this situation. This is would turn out to be my first *A-ha Moment*: my shop chief did not realize that my peers—his subordinates—were the backbone of the whole operation.

Without us, he would not be able to gain any recognition or awards. From that day on, the competitive nature in me established a new target: to be a better leader than my shop chief. I applied to go to the Air Force Academy—the lazy bug was squashed and I would have to start thinking for myself and start seeing the big picture. I mean I had the capability to achieve all I have achieved, but I just chose not to do so the majority of the time. I never got in trouble with the law or did drugs when presented the opportunity; when I was punished, it was mostly due to the fear of a parent's belt, the only thing more frightening than my fear of God. Applying to the Air Force Academy was the best decision I could have made at that time, since I was going to receive a stipend (I was going to be paid to be there) and it was very easy to apply: fill out a form, interview with my commander, and wait for a response. To this day, as a project manager, I look back on that day and have to remind myself that my subordinates are the folks who made my career possible.

The day I received my acceptance letter, I told my commander, who took me off the deployment list to go to Yemen, and I was excited to go. By the time I reported for my shift, I was working swing shift (3:30 p.m. to 11:30 p.m.), the news had reached my shop chief and section chief (the shop chief's boss). They pulled me aside and had me standing at attention while one yelled at me from my left as the other was on my right. At that moment, I knew I had made the right decision. I know I begged to go on this deployment, but I was one of ten who were qualified to go and we had all joined the Air Force for such deployments.

My tenure at the Air Force Academy was typical, with all the social awkwardness when it came to talking to the women I deemed attractive. I became more of a nerd than a smart jock, as I was not able to play on any team, and the courses required a lot of my attention. I am not going to lie—I, like many of my classmates, thought about dropping out. Everybody had their way of motivating themselves to stay. My motivation was to be a better a leader than my former shop chief. I graduated on time without failing any classes, including economics, earning a degree in Aeronautical Engineering. My life's plan was still intact, except for the plan of being married at age 25. My dorky inner player ruined my social life in high school and my chances to achieve a life goal.

After graduating, my time as a commissioned officer was short due to the 2007 force shaping. What many folks do not know about me is that I was suicidal most of the three years following my graduation from the Air Force Academy. I never talked to anybody about this, but my family knew something was wrong—I was lonely and could not talk to the women I wanted to be with, and it put me into a severe depressive state. I tried to be social, but I do not know what it was about me that was off-putting. I was very puzzled. "Perhaps you're trying too hard" was the typical response when I inquired about it. I mean, I was educated, somewhat good-looking, had a career, a car and a house—all the things I thought women wanted in a man. It turned out they were attracted to those things, because I was able to "reach some bases beyond first base," but my inner player was not mature enough to portray the right personality.

I had another *A-ha Moment*: I was in denial about my level of maturity. I had a low level of confidence that I portrayed when I would meet people, but the latter was the overwhelming feeling of just being nervous. So I had to tune in to the nerd in me and start analyzing my conversations and researching body language and start setting tactical goals to achieve my final strategic goal of being married with children before turning 30.

Eventually I gained the confidence to talk to or have an indifferent attitude toward women and not show my dork side. But my darkest hour emerged, and I struck a woman I was seeing after she had slapped me in the midst of an argument. I knew I cared deeply for her, as I would have not gotten angry enough to lay my hands on her, but the ultimate *A-ha Moment* just hit me harder than I had hit her: I was settling.

I was so wrapped up in trying to achieve my goals that I was settling. Yes, she was beautiful and very attractive, but she did not make me a better person—she did the extreme opposite. During the few months I was with her as a couple, I would take three-hour lunch breaks, while I was an officer in the military, just to be with her because she begged me to. She had tried to entice me to steal by sneaking into a movie after leaving a movie we paid to see. She would purposely not do the things I asked her to do because of what she believed; for instance, when she would stay at my house, I would go to bed before her due to our work schedules (she was a waitress and worked the dinner shift). Before going to bed, I'd ask her to turn off all the lights and not leave the television on, as she had done this previously. When I confronted her the next day after she had failed to do what I had requested, her response was that it was not hurting anything and your bill would not be affected since more electricity is spent when you turn things on and off.

To this day, I do not know why I allowed the answer to stand, even if that was the case, which it was not. It was my bill and she was not paying it; I guess I was "twitter-pated" as the owl told Bambi. To make matters worse, she never sincerely apologized for hitting me, as I did multiple times after the incident had occurred. Her feminist reasoning was that men should be able to handle it, but men should never raise their hand to a woman. I know this is not true; as my mother told me, "Nobody has the right to lay their hands on you, and that includes women." So the darkest hour of my life turned to save my life, for God only knows where I would be in life had I returned to that relationship.

I am extremely grateful for the friends I had at that time, for this was the first time I had opened up about what I was going through. When I started seeing women again, I was a different person. I embraced the "I am alone, but not lonely" mentality, and I was able to meet the woman who would become my wife.

The timing was bad from my point of view, as I knew I was going to be force-shaped (the same as being laid off in the civilian world) in a few months because the Air Force had too many engineers, but this did not deter her. The respect I had for her was so great that I did not even try any of the player moves I had developed over the previous year. In fact, it took me three months to even build up the courage to kiss her. I had the perfect cheesy plan: give her a ride to the airport before going to work and give her a departing kiss. Well, we overslept and she had to hurry to the airport and I was going to be late for work, the planned kiss turned out to be a quick peck on the lips. But she was looking out for me even though I wanted to be with her. I mean, I was going to be force-shaped anyway, so what was one act of defiance? She wanted me to be better. I ended up proposing to her within six months of meeting her. I loved her, and I knew she loved me for who I was: a dork.

Bio of Joseph Singleton, MASA

Joseph Singleton was born into a military family. He was born in California, and then lived in North Carolina, North Dakota, Guam, and Washington State. Singleton enjoys playing sports and, as an active member in the community, coaches and referees local youth organizations in addition to high school.

After graduating from high school, Joseph Singleton enlisted in the Air Force and was stationed in Texas for two years. He then graduated from the Air Force Academy after going to the Preparatory School. After serving three years as an officer, Singleton became a project engineer/manager for the Kroger Co. and a contractor for NASA and the Air Force. After earning his master's degree in aeronautical sciences and management, Singleton has over ten years of experience in planning, development, integration, and execution of management functions related to multi-million-dollar programs and projects. He has conducted source selections and monitored multiple contracts from planning/defining needs through construction/deployment by reviewing proposals, awarding contracts, and directing design reviews for software development and construction teams. Mr. Singleton has made a name for himself by creating new or improving established processes to save commercial companies, NASA, and DOD millions of dollars, and will be starting his own IT consulting business within a year.

A-ha Moments
Michael LeClair

My good friend "House"[2] asked me to write an essay for his new compilation of essays on the subject of a defining moment in my life when it became crystal clear which path to take, by whatever discernment, which he has typified as an *A-ha Moment*.

My *A-ha Moment* came when I was about eleven years old. I grew up in the predominately blue-collar town on the east side of Rochester, New York, with the Iroquois name *Irondequoit*. Irondequoit was divided into two school districts: East Irondequoit and West Irondequoit. Nestled between Irondequoit Bay on the east and Rochester on the west, the two Irondequoits were for the most part indistinguishable from Rochester, since the suburban sprawl of house, driveway, house, driveway formed a pattern such that if you blinked and missed the "Welcome to Rochester" sign nine blocks from my house, you would never know you had left Irondequoit.

West Irondequoit was the more affluent of the sisters. The economic makeup included predominantly professional and upper-management Eastman Kodak people, while the poorer sister was mainly the Kodak factory worker, and consequently more conservative. East Irondequoit was made up of a majority of Italian immigrant families with the remainder divided between Irish, Polish, and other eastern European derivations. Set in the

---

2 [Many of the *A-ha Moments* authors call me "House", which is my nickname from high school to college. Whenever someone calls me by that name, I know the time period they entered my life. After 18, I called myself Q Houseman.]

time frame of late 1950s and early 1960s, the norm was bigotry. Racial prejudice was politically correct. Anti-gay sentiments were rampant, resulting in physical violence from teachers as well as the student population on anyone who dared be openly gay. As my high school was 65 to 70% Italian, there was even a more pronounced prejudice: to be Italian made you better than anyone else, but to be Sicilian Italian was better yet than Italian from Naples, Florence, Genoa or any other part of Italy.

Growing up in this extremely ethnically prejudiced environment, it was not inconceivable that my own father would be bigoted. Luckily, he exited from my life at an early age and I was mainly raised by my mother, who was not prejudiced and taught by example to be accepting of all cultures. Unfortunately, being an adolescent pressured by the desire to fit in, yet hampered by the fact that I was of the wrong ethnic background and having no great prowess at sports or possession of monetary wealth, which were the only other mitigating factors, I was definitely not in the "in crowd." There are countless books about adolescent peer pressure and the psychological results brought about by its effect. This sets the stage for my first *A-ha Moment*.

The African-American community in 1962 Rochester was confined, as was the norm in many cities, to an old and rundown part of Rochester on the lower east side. The freedom marches of Dr. King were held in the South, where an argument could be made that race relations were much worse than in the North, but terrible and horrible are only separated by degrees. With the recent killings of unarmed black youth in Florida, Missouri, and Ohio, it is relatively apparent that race relations in America, while better, have not reached the ideals set forth by Dr. King. The pressure built in Rochester, as it did in other communities, until 1964, when the "race riots" (as they were termed) exploded and many of the buildings on Joseph Avenue, the main street in the black enclave, was burned to the ground. The insurance damage was far greater than the much more widely publicized

Watts riots of the same era.

While riding the school bus to junior high school one day in 1962, we were stopped at a signal light, when a school bus from an inner-city school passed in front of us with all the windows covered in plywood. (In retrospect, it was probably a former school bus transformed into some private use.) Sitting in front of me, across from him and across from me were three of the biggest troublemakers in school, who were also some of the best athletes and most popular kids in my class. They immediately started making comments about what the bus from the inner city was doing in our neighborhood. I believe, now, they were baiting to see who they could draw into the discussion and take it a step further.

As I have stated before, adolescent peer pressure is a powerful thing, and totally out of character, I stepped into the trap. I made a derogatory comment using the "N" word, which I had not done before or since. They immediately started to laugh and point at me. I knew my attempt to fit in had backfired, but I did not realize how badly it had transpired, until I realized they were not only pointing at me, but were pointing behind me as well. As I turned around, my eyes met those of the only black kid in my school. The hurt and pain I saw and recognized in his eyes will haunt me forever. I was immediately flooded with shame and the persistent laughing ridicule made it apparent that the three were more than happy, having gotten two birds with one stone. They had caused me to embarrass myself at the cost of shaming the kid behind me.

I do not remember any of the four individuals' names. Within a month, the black kid transferred to another school. I always wondered whether my words were the catalyst for that.

The *A-ha Moment* was now complete. In that small time frame of approximately 45 seconds, I had learned—the hard way—a most valuable lesson. All life is valuable and none is worth more than another. Words can be spoken with devastating results. In those few seconds, my life was changed forever. Bigotry and prejudice were no longer a part of me or my vocabulary. Over the years, I have been rewarded with friendships formed with individuals with different religious backgrounds, sexual orientation, and skin color, all of which would never have happened if I had adopted the prevalent prejudices as my way of life.

Bio of Michael LeClair

I was born February 1, 1951, in Rochester, New York, the last of three children. My due date was April 21, so I spent the first month of my life in an incubator. I attended public school in Irondequoit, New York, and graduated from Eastridge High School. My work history before college includes six years as a paper boy for the Rochester Democrat & Chronicle, working at a Spiegel catalog store, working at Sea Breeze Dreamland Park, working as an order filler at Wards Natural Science Est., and selling snow cones at the Barnum & Bailey Circus, plus playing in my band.

After high school, I attended Marietta College in Marietta ,Ohio. I graduated with a BA in history. While there, I continued playing in bands, worked in the kitchen of the Tau Epsilon Phi fraternity house, and worked in the Calico Bonnet antique store. I also spent four years as the stage manager and two years as the producer of the college's concert series. Some of the bands I hired were the Allman Brothers (Duane's second-to-last performance), the Byrds, the Burrito Bros., Glass Harp, the Mahavishnu Orchestra, and Mountain.

I moved to Oregon, where I got a job with a booking agency and with the passage of a new law allowing bands in taverns, booked some of the best entertainment in Portland. After 12 years booking and being on the road as an audio engineer, I left the music business for a time and had a store on the road to the coast selling pottery made in six studios around Oregon.

Shortly thereafter, I joined another band that lasted 28 years. After 5 years at the store, I got a part-time job at the Yamhill Post Office as a clerk, which grew into my finally ending up as Postmaster of the Yamhill Post Office for the last 10 years. I also spent 10 years as Mayor of Yamhill and 6 years as Municipal Court Judge of Yamhill.

A year ago, I started another band, Lil' Queenie, which just released its first original CD on January 10, 2015.

Moments on the Voyage to Manhood

Gary Carson, JD

Isn't there a Ulysses in every man? Isn't each voyage its own odyssey? Isn't that why Homer's epic still lives in literature, because it lives in each life? Think of Ulysses' voyage not as some ancient travel catalogue, but as a personal journey. The trials he faces are his own and his greatest struggles are within himself. In my own life, I have had to struggle with challenges and seemingly impossible situations, although less grand than Ulysses. You will too.

Ulysses combats pride over and over again—was it not pride that caused him to lead his men to danger in the Cyclops cave? Then, learning little, he taunted Polyphemus to hurl a boulder into his ships. More pride.

He combats the enticements of lust and the sirens sweetly singing. Have we not heard that saccharine song also? He falls under the sway of Circe. He is tempted to forget it all and seek peace in the land of the lotus eaters. Have we not been tempted so?

Sometimes the course will lead you between two bad choices and you must choose the lesser evil. We all have our Straits of Messina.

Like Ulysses, you will not have a chart to guide you, although you will have other tools. The first navigational aid is to know who you are and what your values are, for these are the lodestones of your life. Yes, *your* values, not your parents', your church's, your friends', or your country's values. You must define yourself. You must *locate* yourself on the chart. The "chart" that your parents, school,

OF SUDDEN REALIZATION, INSPIRATION, AND INSIGHT FROM 26 PROFESSIONAL MEN

and church gave you is not real. It is based on many landmarks that may not guide you, but someone else. The first part of the journey is to find *you* without using the chart that your earlier life at home and school provided.

Sometimes personal growth and self-definition come slowly, incrementally, even imperceptibly. Sometimes there are *A-ha Moments*—exclamation points, when the course changes and the sails are retrimmed. Then some new identity or at least a part of an identity emerges.

I have had many more gradual progressions than these *A-ha Moments*. And sometimes I was not even sure such a moment had occurred until later and upon reflection. Was that a red day mark I just passed?

Like many young people, I had been raised with a clear set of values, beliefs, and moral imperatives. There might be some gray areas, but the main life choices were pretty clear cut. God was well defined and had set rules and standards to live by, and was not to be questioned, only understood and obeyed. The United States was also always right and true, and was to be respected and obeyed. There was little room for ambiguity or questioning, and certainly no room for doubt or outright rebellion. But that was before I had begun to choose my own course, not that given by my mother, my church, or my country. Like many, it took some time to reach a point in my life where I was intellectually mature enough to start to question. Like many, at least of my era of the 1960s, that was in the "transition time" between boyhood and manhood. The late teens to mid-20s were a time for such development and maturation then, and I suspect now too. This is the time to learn who you really are and what you really believe, or your compass will be set as it always was as a child.

They are the years when you must examine old beliefs, must feel the discomfort of new roles and new thoughts and new challenges to create *you*. If you do not have this uncomfortable period, this time in the dark when your compass seems to spin, you will likely remain as your parents, your church, your country, and your early friends that formed you. Perhaps then the well-charted course will be you, but you may then never know you are a man in the fullest sense. You will not have defined *your course and yourself*.

Prior to college, I had lived and grown up on our farm on the banks of the Ohio River near Porterfield, Ohio, and in Parkersburg, West Virginia. These places were typical of small towns in the Midwest. The cultural feel was more Midwestern than Appalachian, although Appalachia was an underlayment to the social, economic, and cultural scene. Most people were religious, most Christian, mixed with a very few Jewish people. I'm sure there were atheists and probably many agnostics, but they were not very vocal, nor were they part of the world my mother and I lived in.

My grandmother and my mother raised me, without much reference to a father figure or male role model, except for my uncle. I was often drawn like a moth to him, but only later did I realize it was not just his own fine personality, but it was also attraction to the role model he presented. So one of the fixed points on the chart was the values my mother and grandmother represented.

We lived in a newer, small, brick house on a quite grand old street in town. My mother worked as a school secretary for most of her adult life. It provided her with enough money to support us and gave her summers off so she could be with me and supervise the home. She was not an assertive person, but she was strong in her faith and trusting in people. She raised me in the local Protestant church, where I was duly baptized and attended Sunday school and certainly more church dinners, potlucks, Christmas meals, and other assorted events than I care to remember. I distinctly remember church suppers, when my mother would routinely bring a mixture of cottage cheese, pineapple, and green JELL-O. It still gives me bad memories.

I instinctively realized that I needed to define myself and be my own compass. I had a great female model in my mother, but a limited father model. I felt I would have to invent myself. At times

OF SUDDEN REALIZATION, INSPIRATION, AND INSIGHT FROM 26 PROFESSIONAL MEN

I gendered the quest, but mostly I just wanted to define who I was as a human who just happened to be male. To some extent, I did triangulate off my mother and grandmother. Baseball figures were role models, and this was in an era before performance-enhancing drugs and when stars like Babe Ruth were still presented to children as pure heroes.

One of the early conclusions was that I was NOT an athlete. Some painful physical experiences in gym and intramural games quickly taught me that. Nor was I an artist. I was not good with tools. So maybe I was smart. Maybe I was an "intellectual." I began reading at the Carnegie library, Hardy Boys and even Nancy Drew. Maybe one of the earliest *A-ha Moments* came after a scraped elbow at first base or a mid-thorax hit on the football field!

The first *A-ha Moments* came during my freshman year at Marietta College in 1966. Perhaps the first was a dorm conversation with 'B' from Baltimore. "B" was one of many at Marietta (in the late 1960s) from the US Northeast, and he seemed much more urbane and cosmopolitan than I. He resided in Parsons Hall, as did I. The discussion of God came up, as it often does in dorms (although it surely was the second most common theme). I expressed that there were rules ordained by God and we needed to be cognizant of them. "B" simply said, "Oh, come on now. How can you really believe all that stuff about Big Morris in the sky—we can't eat pork, and we are supposed to reserve a day to do nothing once a week… Have you ever seen Big Morris?" The stark simplicity of his words and his mocking name for God hit home on a small-city guy from West Virginia. In retrospect, there was something about the manner of the expression more than the actual content that started a process of questioning in a way I had not done before. There was the East Coast mindset again!

So when B uttered his words in Parsons Hall… there it was. THE question, presented so matter-of-factly, with a blasé air. It stopped me cold. I drifted away from the conversation and began to think about it. The thinking continues still. And that thinking, that questioning, has shaped much of my life. One of the beacons by which I had triangulated as a very young man had dimmed.

Another moment of change came as a result of Marietta College's dining rules. The college required the freshmen class to dress for dinner: skirts or dresses for the girls and jacket and tie for the boys. It was all quite a proper affair, complete with linen tablecloths. Since this was the mid-1960s, I guess the college felt it was a part of their role to try to instill some rules and acceptable manners to its savage incoming students. It also served to keep the food service company happy.

Since I was still in the mindset that if the proper authorities created rules, they must be obeyed, I did not object. After all, Candide would not question that, in the best of all possible worlds, jackets and ties would be worn to dinner.

But again, an event occurred that seems pretty tame today, but was absolutely groundbreaking. More and more of the students began to grumble. Then they openly complained. Finally, an unlikely spokesman stood up: Schuster, a.k.a. Woody. Woody was a thin, somewhat odd-looking guy that seemed like more of a loner and a bit of a misfit, hardly a Lenin in the lunchroom.

But a sit-in at dinner was organized and, for some reason lost to me, Woody became its spokesman. Tie torn off, atop a table, and waving his blazer like it was a banner of freshman anarchy itself! As I recall, the deans showed up and demanded the tie and jacketless either conform or leave and risk expulsion. The dining hall grew noisy and some left. A boycott of the food service began. Signs were carried. Cliques formed. Protest letters began to be sent to the deans and the campus newsletter. Debates happened. Meaning and portents were sought by many.

Then, a number of weeks later, the Deans backed down—but NO blue jeans. Thus they saved some face, while the false authority of the college was vilified by most of the freshmen.

This pretty trivial protest was another *A-ha Moment*. The

authorities were not always right! They could be challenged! Peaceful protest could produce change. It, of course, was a precursor to the events of the late 1960s and the darkness that was 1970. Never again would there be Blind Faith... except on a music album.

All that had an effect on me. And that was just the beginning, as the anti-Vietnam war protests began. Another point of reference in my high school self-identity had just been obscured. Both of these events happened in freshman year. The change from my high school self may have been triggered by "B" and Woody, but underlying this was the fact that neither was from the mid-Ohio Valley. They were from the East, and I had already been looking to the East, which I saw as more advanced and enlightened than the Midwest.

At night I would listen to my transistor radio and, after all the local radio stations had gone off the air, WABC and Cousin Brucie were still there! In a very silly way, my radio beacon had been located in the East. Although I had chosen to attend Marietta and not go east, Marietta College had brought part of the East to me.

But if the guiding points of religion and established authority had dimmed, the faculty and curriculum at college had provided another kind of structure—not a set of predetermined beliefs to follow, but a process to carry on the course. It stressed using reason and science as tools to determine truth. The path was itself a destination and not some predetermined point. The relativity of truth was also illuminated by my change in major from chemistry to history. Sometimes it remained uncomfortable to continuously confront one's self, the one that had been built on the old black and white values.

The point for you to take away is to not despair or, worse, fall into self-pity when your foundations no longer seem so certain in your "transition time" of the early 20s. Learn who you are and what values you will take to heart. Look for new navigation aids to replace the beacons and lights of your youth. Do not look for answers in drugs or go to the beckoning harpies calling from the rocks. Accept that what may be unsettling at first may in fact be an *A-ha Moment* in the transition to your adult self. Do not be afraid to use new tools to help you define yourself; however, there is seldom a need to completely reject one's past, one's upbringing. They will remain channel markers on your course. In fact, we often go back to some of those same values and traditions—but they are stronger now, for they have been tested, questioned, and have held true to the new YOU that you have created. But forget about the green JELL-O salad!

Bio of Dr. Gary A. Carson

Dr. Carson is an oil and gas land professional currently working at Apache Corporation in San Antonio, Texas. Following a 3-year period of legal practice, he has worked in a variety of land and legal positions during his 38-year career in the domestic oil and gas field, including EDG Resources, Apache Corporation, Pennzoil, Bow Valley Petroleum, and several smaller independents. His work includes the negotiation and drafting of oil and gas leases, other industry contracts, and the supervision of field staff researching land titles and preparing title for drilling. His employment has taken him from his native West Virginia to Denver, Colorado; Tulsa, Oklahoma; and Houston, Corpus Christi, and San Antonio, Texas.

Dr. Carson's educational background includes a BA in history from Marietta College in 1970, graduate studies in European history at Ohio State University, and a JD from Boston College in 1975. Additionally, he studied at the Institute for European Studies in Vienna, Austria, during his junior year. During his collegiate years, he was a member of the Tau Epsilon Phi social fraternity, the APO service fraternity, and a number of campus interest groups.

Dr. Carson and his wife of 38 years, Sue, now reside in Kerrville, Texas, in the Hill Country along with their Pembroke Welsh Corgi and Burmese and Abbysinian cats.

CPSIA information can be obtained
at www.ICGtesting.com
Printed in the USA
FSOW01n0745111017
39770FS